Finding God and Your True Self

Finding God and Your True Self

A DESPERATE JOURNEY

JAMIE OVERHOLSER

Consumed Publishing

Consumed Publishing
An extension of Consumed Ministries
Bloomington MN 55420
www.consumedministries.com

Consumed Ministries exists to share, both in words and actions, that Jesus
Christ desires to give life to the full. We highly value our relationships with
God & people, believing through the context of relationships we can provide
the resources, speaking opportunities, and training to effectively lead people
into the abundant life Jesus promised.

Edited by Delana Peregrim, Jeannie Bernstein, and Paul Wonders
Interior Design and Layout by Gretchen Miller
Cover Design by Julie Overholser
Cover Layout by Eric Beavers
Author Photo courtesy of Shades of Gray Photography
(www.shadesofgraypa.com)

Published in Bloomington, MN by Consumed Publishing
Printed by LuLu Press
Raleigh, NC

Unless otherwise noted, Scripture quotations are from the HOLY BIBLE: New
International Version. Copyright 1973, 1978, 1984 Biblica. Used by permission
of Zondervan Publishing House. All rights reserved.

Other Scripture taken from THE MESSAGE Copyright 1993, 1994, 1995,
1996, 2000, 2001, 2001, 2002. Used by permission of NavPress Publishing
Group.

ISBN: 978-0-9766555-7-2

Library of Congress Control Number: 2011934058

Dedication

To my wife, Julie,
who loves me enough to expose my False Self
and nurture my True Self.
You are beautiful to me.

Table of Contents

Foreword

I first met Jamie in May 2001, when he interviewed for the position of Worship Pastor at the church my wife Deborah and I were attending. He stood on the platform next to a guy playing an acoustic guitar and sang these words:

> *I see the moon, a million stars are out tonight;*
> *Gentle reminders of the way You are.*
> *A sea of glass, a raging storm has come to pass;*
> *You shine Your face in an array of ways.*
> *My feet may venture to the ground,*
> *But You will never let me down.*
> *I can't hold it in.*
> *My soul is screaming: "Hey you, I'm into Jesus!"* (DC Talk)

Something inside of me stirred.

At that time, I had been walking with the Lord for over 15 years. I knew what was in His Word, was respected in our church, and had even taught Sunday School. We always went to church on Sunday morning, Sunday evening, and even Prayer Meeting on Wednesday night. And, of course, we always wore our "Sunday best," because why wouldn't you want God to "see" your best? However, little did I know that other people had referred to me as "unapproachable" and "untouchable." Unbeknownst to me, I had constructed a "false self" that I had been living out of for quite awhile. Not only that, but I had also built a pedestal to place it upon! Even so, something reverberated deep within my soul that day.

Over the next year or so, I got to know Jamie better as he led worship and engaged with us as a pastor. I remember one Friday when Jamie met with me and another friend, Terry. The three of us were leading small groups discussing John Eldredge's book *The Sacred Romance*. Jamie was leading one group, Terry and I the other. It was our practice to meet weekly and discuss the upcoming chapter before getting together with our groups on Sunday night. That week we were talking about Chapter 3: "The Message of the Arrows." Jamie was sitting to my left and Terry to my right, and as our time unfolded we got to a point where these two guys began overflowing with emotion, talking so passionately about God and what He was doing in their lives! Suddenly, I held up my hands for a "time out" and blurted, "I don't get it!" Both of them just smiled, didn't try to explain, but just gently brought the conversation back down to a level where I could relate. Quite frankly, I still didn't "get it," but as we left the restaurant, I felt that familiar stirring in my heart.

It wasn't until the fall of 2002, while I was experiencing the darkest time of my life, that I began to see. Jamie and I made plans one day to have lunch. I was there early, off in a side room with my back to the restaurant reading *Ruthless Trust* by Brennan Manning, a book which Jamie had recommended. As I read, tears began to stream down my cheeks. Jamie came in, saw me, walked over to our table, and as I stood up to hug him, I simply said, "I got it." Jamie showed that all-knowing subtle smile.

The following Sunday as I was "suiting up" as I always had, I looked to check myself in the mirror and I just started to cry. I saw my False Self right there in the mirror looking back at me. I told God then and there I couldn't wear the mask, nor the suit that represented it any longer. That morning, He stripped away my False Self, and I haven't worn a suit to church ever since. It was then He "got me!"

Through all these times and more, the Spirit used Jamie to lead me, guide me, expose my False Self, and direct me towards God—teaching me how to live in the light of my True Self. Jamie's life and words continue to challenge and encourage me, and I have the joy of being part of the "band of brothers" that surrounds and upholds him daily in prayer and action.

This book you are holding contains accounts familiar to me of how God has worked in Jamie's life; stories of how his own False Self has been stripped away, piece by piece, bit by bit. It is an honest accounting of how God has unmasked and molded a man who continues to desperately pursue God. One, like Jacob, who has wrestled with Him in his dark hours and comes away with that inexplicable "something" that ever draws you deeper into the God we love.

My hope is that in these pages you too will feel a "stirring" and allow the Lord of the universe to unmask you to reveal your True Self—the one He intended for you to live out of all along.

Tom Lanton
Dalton, Pennsylvania
Isaiah 26:3

Acknowledgements

This is perhaps the most difficult section of the book to write. Of course, the entire book was written in acknowledgement of how God had His eye on me before the foundation of the world (Ephesians 1:4). No words are adequate to describe the intense gratitude I feel being under His loving gaze and under His protective wing.

I briefly contemplated listing names, but quickly realized that such a feat would be incredibly complex and possibly get me in some proverbial hot water. I've instead decided to acknowledge groups of individuals who have made a profound impact on my life.

To my family (Julie, Charis, Kirsten, Caleb, and Chase) whom I love deeply: thank for encouraging me in this maiden voyage.

To my kindred spirits in the faith: the language of the heart is a beautiful thing.

To the wonderful congregation at The Gathering: you have made shepherding a joy and made healing possible.

To my professors in the MSFL program and my wonderful friends in Cohort #3 at Spring Arbor University (Spring Arbor, MI): God used each of you to spiritually form me in life-changing ways. I love you all.

To my band of brothers down through the years: thank you, men, for walking this wild journey of life with me.

To my Dad and Mom (1937-1999) and three amazing sisters (and their families): God surely had, and continues to have, His hand on our family. To Joan: we can't thank God enough for bringing you to our family.

To all my mentors and teachers: your investment in me has not gone unnoticed.

To the Board of Directors at *The Jacob Institute*: thank you for hearing the call and taking the risk.

To my editors: the editing experience was delightful and humbling. Thank you for being honest and gracious.

To all who encouraged me, provided for me, and prayed for me during this project: you rock!

To the team at Consumed Publishing: thank you for giving a budding author a fighting chance.

And lastly, to all those who are finished splashing around in the shallow end of a generic spirituality, I give you these passionate words:

To a mountain I've not seen
To breath the air so crystal clean
Where I can reach up in the sky
And spread my wings so I can fly
To a land where I've not been
A place where I can dream again
Where I can be as I was meant to be
See as I was meant to see
Oh take me there, take me anywhere but here

Take my hand, and lead me on
Let me know that You are with me all along
Take my heart, and take my fear
Take me anywhere, anywhere but here

I'm not asking for a temporary change in scenery
I'm not looking for a week's vacation from reality
What I need, a transformation that is deeper than the world around me
Reaching to the man inside me
Oh take me there, oh take me there

(Josh and Liz Fronduti, "<u>Anywhere but Here</u>": Used with permission)

"Of making many books there is no end…" (Ecclesiastes 12:12), said Solomon with a sigh. He could have asked, "Why does there have to be so many books?" I've asked myself a thousand times why the world needs another book on God, especially this one. The answer? It doesn't. The world doesn't *need* this book, or any other humanly composed book for that matter, to find God. People were finding God long before any books were written about Him. Yet I find myself mysteriously drawn to the same world that is somewhat unsettling to me—the world of authorship and books. Now don't get me wrong, I love books. I own lots of them and love to read. I have my favorite authors, and I love to write. However, when I peruse the shelves at Barnes and Noble or the local Christian bookstore, I end up asking questions like these: Do we really need a book on *that*? Is *that* the key to the Christian life? What does *this* author have to say that the others haven't said already? Who does this guy think he is anyway?

Now I'm going to throw this book into the fray of a market that is more crowded than ever before. Over one million books were published in the United States in 2009 alone according to Bowker (the world's leading source for bibliographic information). At least two-thirds of these books were self-published. I guess Solomon was right.

Generations ago books were generally written by experts and really smart individuals. Today anyone can write a book, and the author doesn't necessarily have to be an expert or intelligent or even human. Kermit the Frog wrote a book on life's greatest lessons! So who do I think I am joining this vast array of opinions and beliefs about God that in the long run will have little effect on humanity? Here's my short answer. I'm not attempting to affect humanity, but perhaps God will use me to affect *you*. If *you* can glean just one crucial aspect about God and your True Self from my story, I will consider this book worth the paper it's printed on or the hard drive space it takes up on your e-reader.

Writing a book is risky. Putting my honest thoughts and current beliefs in print runs the risk of creating an identity that can never be changed. I trust that you, the reader, will give me the grace and flexibility to learn and grow as a fumbling apprentice of Jesus, as well as a budding author. This journey of spiritual formation is an evolution of sorts that includes progression and regression, successes and failures, mountains and valleys, consolations and desolations, faith and doubt, bright mornings and dark nights, and everything in between. I will give you the same respect and understanding as you allow Christ to be formed in you. If we're honest with ourselves, we have to admit that the resignation of our False Self and the resurrection of our True Self are much harder than we ever thought.

The following pages chronicle my desperation and God's irresistible romancing of my heart. My journey has taken me from a belief that I know almost everything about God to the realization that I know very little.

In all honesty, I catch brief but concentrated glimpses of God. My driving passion is to escort you to the very heart of God, to show you Jesus, and in the end attempt to awaken you to God and your True Self.

Except for the first few chapters there is no apparent, logical progression. The chapters do not necessarily build on each other. I simply take the subject at hand—*Finding God and Your True Self*—and look at it from several different angles and perspectives. I may actually raise more questions than I answer. This may unnerve you. My goal is to have you interact, think, and feel rather than simply accept my spin on these spiritual concepts. My intention is not to provide a "how-to" manual for the Christian life, but to offer a glimpse into what it means to know God intimately. My words will be a healing balm for many, an utter mystery to others, and heresy to a handful.

I am indebted to several men and women whose writings have enabled me to find my heart. John Eldredge, Brent Curtis, Brennan Manning, Susan Muto, Larry Crabb, Frederick Buechner, Kathleen Norris, Henri Nouwen, A. W. Tozer, Michael Yaconelli, G. K. Chesterton, Oswald Chambers, and John Eagan possess an awareness of God that supersedes modern theological bounds. They have unknowingly guided me through the mysterious territory of God's heart. Portions of what I will attempt to communicate are a result of what I've learned from these individuals. Remember, there's nothing new under the sun. I do not claim to have found what has not already been found by countless Christ followers. I've simply found it for myself. And so must you.

Lastly, I write the following pages in the spirit of Henri Nouwen who admittedly did not completely grasp or live fully the thoughts and truths contained in his books. In fact, from time to time I will reread what I wrote months ago and struggle with believing it. Not because I think it's wrong, but because I find it incredibly difficult to live. In the words of a friend, these truths need to be "re-read, re-learned, turned over, and re-worked" in such a way that keeps me sensitive as I walk this spiritual path of finding God and my True Self.

Jamie Overholser
Clarks Summit, Pennsylvania
In the year of our Lord two thousand and eleven

1

God and His first words

"In the beginning God…" (Genesis 1:1). He is "the Alpha and Omega…who is, and who was, and who is to come, the Almighty" (Revelation 1:8). I believe by faith that God exists and that we can find Him.

As God pulls the curtain to expose the stage on which all of humanity will play a part, He speaks, "Let there be light" (Genesis 1:3). These are His very first words. Have we ever truly contemplated the significance of what God chose to say *first*? When God could have selected *anything* to say, why did He choose these words? Why did He not say, "Look, here I am. I'm God!"? Why did He say, "Let there be light."?

Through the centuries, the ancient Greeks and men such as Sir Isaac Newton, Christian Huychens, James Maxwell, Max Plank, and Albert Einstein have tried to give definition to light. Current definitions of light include words and phrases like these:

"Electromagnetic radiation that has a wavelength in the range from about 4,000 (violet) to about 7,700 (red) angstroms and may be perceived by the normal unaided human eye."

"That agent, force, or action in nature by the operation of which upon the organs of sight, objects are rendered visible or luminous."

"Something that makes vision possible."

"The sensation aroused by stimulation of the visual receptors."

"The form of electromagnetic radiation that acts upon the retina of the eye and optic nerve making sight possible."

Sources of light include the sun, a light bulb, fire, a flashlight, lightning, and the gleam in the eye of a little child. Light seems pretty...scientific. We enjoy the benefits of its existence and are annoyed when certain sources of light fail to give us the warmth and illumination we desire.

But if you take even two or three minutes and try to comprehend the *concept* of light, it just may border on incomprehensible, especially in the context of Genesis 1:3. "And God said, 'Let there be light,' and there was light." All of a sudden there was "*electromagnetic radiation that has a wavelength in the range from about 4,000 (violet) to about 7,700 (red) angstroms and may be perceived by the normal unaided human eye.*" What makes this creation of light even more amazing is when you realize—are you ready for this?—*the sun had not yet been created.* Genesis 1:14-16 say, "And God said, 'Let there be lights in the expanse of the sky to separate the day from the night, and let them serve as signs to mark seasons and days and years, and let them be lights in the expanse of the sky to give light on the earth.' And it was so. God made two great lights—the greater light to govern the day and the lesser light to govern the night." "Light" in Genesis 1:3 is an essence separate from the sun. Just let that mystery settle in for a moment. Try to conceive of light that has no known source. It's astonishing since we normally associate light with some object of origin such as the sun or a light bulb or fire. I offer no practical application at this point other than realizing that God immediately bewilders us with who He is.

In the definitions of light that I cited earlier, there is a common thread: light is a force that allows the eyes to see. It makes vision possible. It stimulates the visual receptors. It acts upon the retina and the optic nerve. It renders objects visible. When God said, "Let there be light," could it be that He was saying, "Let there be the ability to see."? *Let there be the ability to perceive and understand what is going on around us. Let there be the ability to soak it all in.* You see, God didn't create everything in the dark and then turn the lights on. He created light first because light was absolutely necessary to the entire creative process. Beyond that, *light is necessary for the whole living process.* Through science we know that light is necessary for growth – whether vegetation, animal life, or human life. Life cannot be sustained in total darkness. Living things would start to shrivel up and die if they were in the dark too long; mentioning nothing of what it would do to the psyche of a human being.

Even as God created the heavens and the earth, Genesis 1:2 says that "the earth was formless and empty, darkness was over the surface of the deep." In the dark everything was shapeless and unfilled. Then God said, "We need light" (my paraphrase). Light was (is) the change agent.

Isaiah 9:2 declares that "the people walking in darkness have seen a great light; on those living in the land of the shadow of death a light has dawned." The physical earth was not the only thing that was ever trapped in the dark; "people" are now in the dark. This description not only describes the state of the people of God during the days of Isaiah, it describes the condition of humankind without God. We're in the dark and we're living "in the land of the shadow of death." This verse is actually in the context of the prophecy concerning the coming of Jesus to this earth the first time. It poetically describes what *needs* to happen, what *has* to happen, what *will* happen, and from our perspective what *has already* happened for countless people – they've seen a great light, a light has dawned.

Have you ever thought of the different reactions we have to light? How does a teenage boy react when his dad comes into his room in the morning and turns on the lights and pushes open the curtains? How will the people in the flood ravaged regions of the earth feel when the rain stops and the sun shines again? How do burglars respond to the search light of the police?

How do people who are lost at sea react to the search light of an approaching aircraft? How do you feel when you're on the beach and you feel the warmth and sense the invigorating energy of the sun? Depending on the situation and the source of light, we can respond differently.

I had an experience a couple weeks ago that happens at least two or three times a year, especially during the winter months. There was just enough precipitation and dirt on my windshield that I needed to clear it off, but my Jeep was out of windshield washer fluid. I attempted to clear my windshield by just turning on the wipers. Well, you know what happened. The windshield became one big smudge. To add insult to injury, it was a bright sunny day! During the winter months the sun stays a bit lower in the sky and has the ability to be in the wrong place at the wrong time. It wouldn't have been so bad if my windshield had not been one big smudge. And you know what happens when you catch the sun at just the wrong angle with a smudged windshield, right? You can't see! Do you know what my first reaction was? *Stupid sun!*

Usually when we have a negative reaction to light, it is not the light's fault. It's usually something that we have done or not done that causes us to curse the light when we should be examining why we're having such a negative reaction to it. I'm reminded of bus trips when I was a teenager. Usually the scenario was something like this: we're coming home late at night from a youth group trip to Cedar Point or traveling home from camp. For some reason our youth pastor or the bus driver would just randomly turn on the lights inside the entire bus. When that happened, everyone, especially the couples sitting together near the back, would immediately sit up straight and start discussing the finer points of theology!

We have a choice to either bless the light or curse it. We can embrace the light or reject it. We can choose to understand how the light is trying to guide us or we can refuse to understand the role of light in our lives. When I express it that way, you're probably realizing that I'm not talking about physical light any longer. I'm talking about that light in Isaiah that has dawned. What exactly is that light?

In John 1:4 we read a description of Jesus: "In him was life, and that life was the light of men." The original concept here for light actually im-

plies "the effulgence [radiance] of God's glory."[1] Jesus as light is God's
way of bringing Himself into each of our lives. In verse 5 we read that
"the light shines in the darkness, but the darkness has not understood it."
The darkness just doesn't "get it." It doesn't comprehend or understand,
or doesn't *want* to understand how the radiance of divine light is useful or
helpful or formational. To darkness, light just seems like a big nuisance or
intrusion.

Jesus expressed it this way in John 3:19, "This is the verdict: Light has
come into the world, but men loved darkness instead of light because their
deeds were evil." The essence of the divine has come into the world—
your world, my world, your day, my day, your reality, my reality—and Jesus
exposes the reason why some of us squint our eyes and hold our hands up
to our face, turning our heads as we scream *Nooooooo!* The reason? We'd
rather be in darkness. Why? Because we love it. Why do we love it?
Because the darkness covers up what's really going on, what Jesus
describes as evil. *Evil?*

Here we go again. We see the same thread time and time again in this
story the Scripture is telling. It's another attempt at what the human race
has done since the time Adam and Eve betrayed God in the garden. We
hide. And the easiest place to hide is in the dark. The reason we do not
understand the light or accept the light is because the light exposes us, and
we don't want to be exposed. Instead of being surrounded by the radiance
of God's glory, we pull the cover over our heads. We sew our fig leaves
together, and hide in the bushes where it's dark. You see, in the dark it's
much easier to maintain our False Selves, and to live the life of Mr. Imposter and Miss Poser. (I will unpack more fully the concepts of the False
Self and True Self in chapter 2).

John 3:20 says, "Everyone who does evil hates the light, and will not
come into the light for fear that his deeds will be exposed." I'm not making this stuff up. Jesus gently explains this concept to a man named Nicodemus who—ironically—came to Him under the cover of darkness (See
John 3:2). Jesus is reviewing how we humans naturally react. We don't,

however, *have* to react that way. He goes on to explain that "whoever lives by the truth comes into the light, so that it may be *seen plainly* that what he has done has been done through God" (emphasis mine). The light—the radiant essence of God Himself—is now synonymous with truth. Jesus asks Nicodemus (and you and me) to voluntarily "come into the light" so that everything can be "seen plainly." Remember the original purpose of light? It allows our eyes to be able to see.

We can either be exposed by the light against our will or we can willingly step into the light and into the truth about ourselves. It is the difference between having our False Selves exposed or having our True Selves illuminated. The latter is less painful. The light is not our enemy, though the real enemy would like you to believe otherwise. Our real enemy—Satan himself—knows that if he can keep you in the dark long enough, you will shrivel up and die. The goal is to step into the light (and eventually live there) often so that it's not such a jolt to our system when we do. In other words, don't live in the dark so long that you can't handle the light (the truth) when it comes along.

Here's a very practical way that I use to stay exposed to the light. There are two or three men in my life who have permission to tell me when they think I'm in the dark, when they think I'm living far too much out of my False Self, when they see deeds that are evil, when they sense a wrong attitude in me, or when they see that I'm just not tracking with God like I need to be. They know me well enough to see right through me, and they ask questions that expose me. Not out of judgment, but out of love; not from what we traditionally know as "accountability," but from true spiritual community. False Selves live in isolation or pseudo-community. They will either cut themselves off from spiritual influencers or create shallow relationships that keep them socially connected, but at a safe distance from anyone that might have the ability to see deep into their soul. Darkness more befits the False Self.

Let me reinforce that God is not trying to be cruel with this concept of light. The spiritual invasion of "the all-glorious divinity"[2] and the truth He brings should bring utter relief to a soul trapped in darkness. Light allows God to creatively form us into the image of His Son, and also allows us to really live and experience the transformational change that light encourages. Light is that change agent that begins to shape a new identity—the True Self.

As it was in the beginning, so shall it be when God's Kingdom is established on the earth. When Paradise returns, "the city does not need the sun or the moon to shine on it, for the glory of God gives it light" (Revelation 21:23). "There will be no more night. They will not need the light of a lamp or the light of the sun, for the Lord God will give them light" (Revelation 22:5). "Let there be light" are the very first words we hear from God, and light will emanate from Jesus Himself for all eternity. From beginning to end "he wraps himself in light" (Psalm 104:2) and desires to enfold us in "the brightness of his presence" (Psalm 18:12).

With all your heart

There's a phenomenon that happens between mothers and their children. It happened to me when I was a kid and it terrified me every time. My mother would ask me to go to a certain location in the house or the garage or the basement to find something for her. The request went something like this: "Jamie, go to the basement and find me that 'blah-blah-blah' on the top shelf by the freezer." I knew instantly that it wouldn't be there. It was probably there when she was telling me to go find it, but I was certain that as soon as I started descending the steps to the basement, it would disappear. More often than not I would spend what seemed like hours looking at that shelf for whatever she wanted and I would not be able to find it. I would traipse back up the steps and with fear and trepidation let the following words dribble from my lips: "It's not there; I can't find it." My mom (and every other mother in America) would utter something like "If I have to go down there…" or "Just because you can't find it doesn't mean it's not there." Well, of course, she would go down there, and wouldn't you know it, as soon as she started to descend the steps the object would miraculously reappear on the shelf. If moms knew this was going to happen every time, why didn't they just go get the darn thing for themselves in the first place? Finding an object in the basement is not always easy. Finding God is sometimes even harder.

God said, "You will seek me and find me when you seek me with all your heart" (Jeremiah 29:13). Although God is neither lost nor hidden, at times, from our human perspective, He will seem to us as if He has been veiled or concealed. Simply peruse the Psalms and hear the anguished cries of those searching for God: "Answer me when I call you, O my righteous God" (Psalm 4:1). "Why, O LORD, do you stand far off? Why do you hide yourself in times of trouble?" (Psalm 10:1). "How long, O LORD? Will you forget me forever? How long will you hide your face from me?" (Psalm 13:1). The reality of life with its times of trouble *will* cause a dense fog to settle in and obscure our vision of God. As dark storm clouds almost completely block the sun's rays and warmth, so can the bizarre and demonic circumstances of life almost completely obscure the magnificent light that is God. Bank on it. It *will* happen. The psalmist David was honest about it and we should be, too. But beware: the religious False Self will rise up and try to "buck up" under the pressure. He or she will try to convince you that allowing that dense fog to blur your vision is a sign of weakness and possible carnality, but don't let him or her fool you. Life *is* hard and God *does seem* far away at times.

Now, to be fair, the fog will be less dense for some than for others. Sometimes trouble actually invites a genuine increased presence of the reality of God rather than distance. Consider this a gift and a grace. There are, however, those who will choose first to echo the words of David in frantic fashion. This is when we must also plunge ourselves headlong into seeking and finding that pinhole of light that will give us some sense of perspective and sanity. In these times of trouble, it *is* possible to seek God out and find Him, to turn on the low beams and crawl our way slowly through the heavy mist, white knuckled and tense. We can't simply give up and put out the clarion call to "come out, come out wherever You are." It's not as easy as the childhood game makes it out to be.

It takes heart to do anything worthwhile, and finding God is no different. God said, "You will...find me when you seek me with *all your heart*" (emphasis mine). We will never find God with our "own understanding" (Proverbs 3:5). Our intellect and powers of reason are no match for a God who, many times, defies explanation. Of course, there are certain characteristics and activities of God that we attempt to explain in a theological sense, but if we are honest with ourselves these efforts fall terribly short in trying to explain "things [we] do not understand, things too wonderful for [us] to know" (Job 42:3). We think we know; we think we understand, until we hear the same thunderous voice that Job heard that says, "Brace yourself like a man..." (Job 38:3). It is then, and only then, that we realize that finding God may be more challenging than we originally thought, that finding God takes a person who is willing to pour his or her heart into it. Jesus said, "In this world you will have trouble. But take heart!" (John 16:33). The reality, however, is that many actually lose heart in those times of trouble, and when a person loses heart he or she also loses the very essence needed to seek and find God. The enemy of our soul knows the very target he must hit in order to cripple our pursuit of God—the heart. If through trouble he can make us lose heart, he has also disabled our ability to seek and find the One who has "overcome the world" (John 16:33).

The heart is our spiritual core (or center). It's capable of doing many things according to the Scriptures. All belief, faith, trust, work, commitment, love, and desire stem from the heart, just to name a few. When the heart is wounded it affects our ability to trust. When our heart has been assaulted and hurt deeply, we may not be able to muster the energy to go to work. If our spiritual core or center has been hit, we may start to question everything. If our heart has been broken by someone or some event, we may lose all desire; no one may be able to stir us. We may actually feel like God has abandoned us, so we no longer seek Him like we used to.

Take Marcy (not her real name) for example. She has a rare cancer that has her doctors shaking their heads. For the last year and a half she has stared death in the face. It's frightening to say the least. Her uncommon cancer puts her in the 1% of all cancer patients. It goes without saying that her torment has not just been physical, but emotional, relational, and yes, even spiritual.

Meet Brian (not his real name). He's a single man in his forties who is struggling to make sense of the current realities in his life. He *thought* he heard God and followed where he *thought* the Spirit was leading him. But now he is at the point of, in his own words, "questioning everything…my current status in life, my faith, my future, all of it." He goes on to say, "I am not truly a part of anyone's life outside the church [service]."

Lindsay (not her real name) is in her third year at a Christian college. While enjoying a cup of coffee and catching up on some reading at a local restaurant this morning, I ran into her. I have to hand it to her. She could have easily slapped on the happy face (the False Self) and engaged in shallow trivialities, but she didn't. She could not hide the tears as she said, "Mr. O, I'm struggling."

Marcy, Brian, and Lindsay represent us all. If we're honest, each of us is struggling with something just under the surface. Along with Job (from the book of Job in the Old Testament) each one of us struggles to move from "my ears had heard of you" (Job 42:5a) to "but now my eyes have seen you" (Job 42:5b). The catch is that it will most likely take a heart of perseverance to journey through trouble in this life. As Henri Nouwen said in his book *Life of the Beloved*, "The first step in healing is not a step away from the pain, but a step toward it."[3]

When we step toward our pain, we also move toward the possibility of those transcendent moments when God shows up unannounced and floods us with His divine presence. This is the mystical side of our relationship with God—what Tony Campolo and Mary Albert Darling call "transcendent intimacy."[4] A.W. Tozer describes the Christian mystic as the one who "experiences his faith down in the depths of his sentient being"[5] and one who is "quietly, deeply, and sometimes almost ecstatically aware of the Presence of God in his own nature and in the world around him."[6] Perhaps you've had a burning bush or Mount of Transfiguration experience where you want to take off your shoes, build permanent living quarters, and never leave. Maybe you've had extended periods where you've experienced the gracious Presence of God and "know this love that surpasses knowledge" (Ephesians 3:19). There is no doubt that we long to lunge toward Jesus and cling to Him as Mary did in the garden after His resurrection. But as Oswald Chambers admitted in the October 1st entry of *My Utmost for His Highest*, "The moments on the mountain tops are rare moments."[7] He continues, "We are not built for the mountains and the dawns and the aesthetic affinities, those are for moments of inspiration; that is all. We are built for the valley, for the ordinary stuff we are in, and that is where we have to prove our mettle."[8] As wonderful as it is for God to find us in those transcendent moments, we need God in "the ordinary stuff," in the hard stuff, in the events of life that threaten our resolve and attempt to silence the Voice that says, "I will never leave you nor forsake you. Be strong and courageous." (Joshua 1:5b-6a).

There is no doubt that God relentlessly pursues humankind in ways that go far beyond what is humanly reasonable. As we will see in a later chapter, trouble does not negate God's love for us. There is nothing that can separate us from His love. He will continue to pursue us in the midst of our pain, in the midst of prodigal tendencies. There is, however, an aspect of our relationship with Him in which *He* desires to be pursued as well. He wants *us* to come running after *Him*. He wants *us* to make the long, hard journey home. God desires reciprocity in this love relationship just like any human lover wants a response to his or her love. We not only seek God out when we need refuge and strength, we seek God and find Him as a response to, as Brent Curtis and John Eldredge define it, this "sacred romance" we're in.

As we persevere to seek and find God, our mothers' admonition has a spiritual quality to it: "Just because you can't find it doesn't mean it's not there." Likewise, just because we can't find God doesn't mean He's not there. God is always *there*. Just as "the bread of the Presence" (Exodus 25:30) was always on the table in the Old Testament tabernacle, so God is always before us, offering us His Presence and divine sustenance. He *is* there, but perhaps only our ears have heard, and our eyes have not yet seen. This is why the apostle Paul prays "that the eyes of your heart may be enlightened" (Ephesians 1:18).

The words of our mothers continue to have spiritual significance: "You may have to move something to find it." In other words, did you *really* look? I confess that I would just stand there and stare. If the thing didn't jump out at me, I would swear it wasn't there. Deuteronomy 4:29 says, "You will find him if you *look* for him with all your heart and with all your soul" (emphasis mine). Some of us claim that we can't find God because we really don't *want* to find Him. We're scared of what we'll find when we do. This is due mostly to a sorely inaccurate perception of God. We don't want to find the God of our parents' religion or the God of our youth. We don't want to find the God of our ecclesiastical denomination or the God of no fun and no sex. And we especially don't want to find the God who will take all our money. So we don't bother looking. We don't bother "moving something," like our own biases and hang-ups that just may very well be hiding who God *really* is. Our own distorted image of God has provided a seemingly legitimate excuse for calling off the search. *Who wants to find a God like that?*

The Scriptures reveal what we will truly find when we find God: strength (1 Samuel 23:16), refuge (Psalm 91:4), rest for our souls (Jeremiah 6:16), life (Matthew 16:25), great delight (Psalm 112:1), peace (John 14:27), wisdom (James 1:5), love and fullness (Ephesians 3:14-19), beauty (Psalm 27:4), good news and healing (Isaiah 61:1), freedom and sight (Luke 4:18), and a Savior (Luke 1:47). We'll also find some things that perhaps we weren't expecting: a consuming fire (Hebrews 12:29), the Dread Warrior of Heaven (Revelation 19:11-16), sheer and utter holiness (Isaiah 6:3), the Fear (Genesis 31:42, 53), and the Creator (Genesis 1:1), just to name a few.

Why? Why push through? Why seek and find God? Why go down the road less traveled? Why choose the narrow road as opposed to the wide road? Why choose *this* God instead of all those other gods? Why take the risk of putting your heart out there and getting it broken? Why walk by faith and not by sight? Wouldn't it be easier and a lot more fun to "eat, drink, and be merry" (Luke 12:19)?

To eat, drink, and be merry is to conclude that there is nothing beyond us—that life is all about me. And yes, to be completely honest, it would be much easier and a lot more fun—from the perspective of the False Self. Take a look around at those who pursue life to the exclusion of God. Many of them are having a downright blast! A momentary blast, but a blast nonetheless. However, their extreme nearsightedness keeps them trapped in a futile search for life in things that aren't life-giving. Thrill-giving perhaps, but not life-giving. In the end, if they're honest, the blast feels more like an explosion. Jesus said that "life does not consist in the abundance of...possessions" (Luke 12:15). Since true life is found outside the material and temporal, we must search for the spiritual and the eternal.

To search for and find God is to conclude that there *is* Someone beyond you; that you are not the center of the universe; that life, though it contains elements of the material and temporal, must also exist in the dimensions of the spiritual and eternal. Certainly God has "set eternity in the hearts of men" (Ecclesiastes 3:11).

Whether we realize it or not, humankind has been searching for God since the beginning. The tragedy is when we find *a god* instead of *God*. When we find *a god*, the search for *God* ends, or is at least severely disrupted. We become enamored with and play with this *god* as if we've found the real thing. This *god*, or idol, is subtle and dangerous. In his book *The Peace Making Pastor*, Alfred Poirier points out that "counterfeit gods...are lawgivers. They command us. They shape our affections, direct our decisions, and motivate our behavior."[9] Simply stated, when we find *a god* our False Self is conceived and begins to grow. Do you see it? This *god* or idol has the power to "shape our affections, direct our decisions, and motivate our behavior." A false *god* is the breeding ground for the False Self. It's almost as if we no longer control ourselves.

Do you see why it is imperative that we find *God?*

---

[1] Spiros Zodhiates, editor, *The Complete Word Study Dictionary: New Testament* (Iowa Falls, IA: World Bible Publishers, 1992), p. 208.

[2] Ibid.

[3] Henri Nouwen, *Life of the Beloved* (New York: The Crossroad Publishing Company, 1992), p. 93.

[4] Tony Campolo and Mary Albert Darling, *The God of Intimacy and Action* (San Francisco: Jossey-Bass, 2007), p. 4.

[5] A.W. Tozer, *The Christian Book of Mystical Verse* (Harrisburg, PA: Christian Publications, 1963), p. vi.

[6] Ibid.

[7] Oswald Chambers, *My Utmost for His Highest* (London, Edinburgh: Marshall, Morgan & Scott, 1927), p. 275.

[8] Ibid.

[9] Alfred Poirier, *The Peace Making Pastor* (Grand Rapids, MI: Baker Books, 2006), p. 59.

2

My Prayer

Jesus, I feel completely inadequate writing this chapter. Most of the time I'm terribly confused about my own self. Am I really living from my True Self or is my False Self just a really good actor? There are times when I feel like Dr. Jekyll and Mr. Hyde spiritually. Writing and speaking about this stuff does not miraculously make it true in my own life. So many times I've wanted to bag this whole project because I feel so incredibly unworthy of guiding others when I don't know where I'm headed half the time.

In the spirit of Tozer, "I want to want Thee." My soul yearns for You, Lord, but it also yearns for other things—revenge, a nicer car, a trouble-free life, and validation from others. I say (and sing) that You are "more than enough" for me, but when I have the option to choose You above all others, why do I sometimes not choose You? Why do the demonic minions nip at my heels? And why don't I kick them to the side in disgust? Why is there a part of my heart that cannot live without the recognition of others? Why do my feelings get hurt so easily? Why, deep down inside, do I care so much about what others think and say about me? Why do I want others to like me and to think that I bring something significant to the table of their lives? And why do I want others to see and applaud my strengths while turning a blind eye to my many weaknesses? This is nothing more than selfishness wrapped in self-pity. Are You really enough for me?

Lord, You recently wrenched from my grip position, title, security, and influence. Like dust in Your hand You blew away years of relationships that are no more. There were those who were among my band of brothers that are now mere shadows and memories. With David I concur: "If an enemy were insulting me I could endure it; if a foe were raising himself against me, I could hide from him. But it is you, a man like myself, my companion, my close friend, with whom I once enjoyed sweet fellowship as we walked with the throng at the house of God" (Psalm 55:12-14).

In an instant You changed the course of my life without warning. In Your divine wisdom You ripped away an identity that was comfortable and familiar, but one that no longer fit. You knocked the props out from under me and asked me to stand with only You holding me up. Only You. You. You asked me to live what I had talked about for so long. With great personal pain You've escorted me into the next stage of the journey. I failed to jump, so You pushed. Nice one. Touché. Although I never want to go through these days again, the struggle has led to greater union and intimacy. You are peeling away my False Self layer by layer and leaving my heart exposed and naked to the harsh elements of reality and to the warm glow of the Radiant Son. But You are also re-clothing me with Your Spirit and slowly but surely forming Yourself inside me. You do some of your best work through pain.

Potter, I am the clay. Pound me. Shape me. Mold me. Shepherd, I am Your little helpless lamb. Lead me. Guide me. Protect and rescue me. Master, I am Your servant. Command me and I will do Your bidding. Father, I am Your child. Hold me. Discipline me in Your love. Father me. Friend, it is an honor to be called Your friend. Stick with me closer than a brother. Lover, I am Your Beloved Bride. Ravish me. May there be no other but You.

Almighty God, I am my Truest Self when I am the surrendered clay, the helpless and innocent lamb, the loyal servant, the obedient child, the faithful friend, and the radiant Beloved.

Jacob, my unlikely hero

The story of Jacob in the Old Testament has captured my heart. With double-edged precision the life of Jacob mirrors many, if not all, of our stories. Here's why. Throughout his life Jacob couldn't quite own up to the

Imposter or the Poser inside. He hid behind his False Self tricking and deceiving others to push his own personal agenda in life.

Jacob was the son of Isaac and the grandson of Abraham. Jacob had a twin brother, Esau, who was not identical—in fact they were quite opposite in almost everything. The actual birth of these boys was quite symbolic. They came from Rebekah's womb with Jacob grasping at the heel of Esau. This was indicative of the way Jacob would lean in life. In fact the name Jacob literally means "grasping at the heel." This "grasping" would manifest itself symbolically by turning Jacob into the common synonyms for his name: Cheater, Trickster, Schemer, and Manipulator. In fact, the word "deceitful" in the Old Testament, (e.g. Jeremiah 17:9) actually comes from a root word meaning "tripping up insidiously by the heel."[1]

In the Genesis account of Jacob's life, it's interesting to note that there were two significant occasions when Jacob refused to give his name and offer his real identity. The first situation, found in Genesis 27, came just after Jacob had tricked Esau into selling him his birthright. In that day there were certain rights that Esau had because he was born first and that included a patriarchal blessing from Isaac his father that would set all of the other rights into motion. So Jacob, having bought the birthright from Esau with a simple bowl of soup, disguised himself as Esau, went to Isaac (who's going blind), and asked for the blessing. Because Isaac heard Jacob's voice, he asked, "Who is it?" Jacob said to his father, "I am Esau your firstborn." Then a few verses later Isaac asked again because he felt and smelled Esau, but the voice was still Jacob's. "Are you really my son Esau?" he asked. "I am," Jacob replied. Had Jacob uttered his real name, it would have been an admission of guilt in more ways than one. The phrases "I am Jacob" and "I am deceitful" were more interchangeable than ever in that moment.

Jacob was again tight-lipped about his real identity when he headed back east to where his family originally came from in search of a wife. When he came across a woman named Rachel, Genesis 29:12 says, "He had told Rachel that he was a relative of her father and a son of Rebekah."

But he didn't say his name. Now, Jacob wasn't altogether stupid here. What guy in his right mind when meeting a beautiful single woman would say, "Hello beautiful, my name is Cheater. I love you and want you to be my wife, but just realize that I may betray you someday"? Nonetheless, Jacob was still unwilling to come to grips with who he was, what was lodged deep in his heart, and how he'd been manipulating people his whole life. The entire story of Jacob's marriage to Rachel will have to wait for another time, but about twenty years later Jacob returned to where he was born. He realized that he would have to meet up with Esau at some point, and wondered if his twin brother was still angry with him. But before that happened God had something up His sleeve—an impromptu wrestling match to be exact. Here is the way Frederick Buechner describes it in his book *The Magnificent Defeat*:

> And then it happens. Out of the deep of the night a stranger leaps. He hurls himself at Jacob, and they fall to the ground, their bodies lashing through the darkness. It is terrible enough not to see the attacker's face, and his strength is more terrible still, the strength of more than a man. All the night through they struggle in silence until just before morning when it looks as though a miracle might happen. Jacob is winning. The stranger cries out to be set free before the sun rises. Then, suddenly, all is reversed.

> He merely touches the hollow of Jacob's thigh, and in a moment Jacob is lying there crippled and helpless. The sense we have, which Jacob must have had as well, is that the whole battle was from the beginning fated to end this way, that the stranger had simply held back until now, letting Jacob exert all his strength and almost win so that when he was defeated, he would know that he was truly defeated; so that he would know that not all the shrewdness, will, brute force that he could muster were enough to win. Jacob will not release his grip,

only now it is a grip not of violence but of need, like the grip of a drowning man.

The darkness has faded just enough so that for the first time he can dimly see his opponent's face. And what he sees is something more terrible than the face of death—the face of love. At last he cries out, 'I will not let you go, unless you bless me!' Not a blessing that he can have now by the strength of his cunning or the force of his will, but a blessing that he can have only as a gift.[2]

After the skirmish with God was over, Jacob was asked the one question he'd been avoiding all his life; "What is your name?" God asked. "Jacob," he answered. R. Paul Stevens makes a keen observation here: "Jacob must be himself before God…not even the Jacob he would like to be."[3]

The Jacob in us all

We all have the tendency, if we're honest, to continue the strategy of hiding that was passed down to us by Adam and Eve. We hide, cover up, and create an attractive "fig leaf" that promotes self and stiff-arms God. And the very fact that we may not believe this about ourselves may indicate just how comfortable we are in the skin of the Imposter. With George MacDonald we must admit every day that "every morn my life afresh must break the Crust of self, gathered about me fresh."[4]

In order to live full and wholly in the True Self, we have to come to grips with our inner complexity. In the Christian tradition in which I grew up we regularly sang a song at the end of every worship service called *Just As I Am*. It may seem hard to believe, but God doesn't want you any other way. He asks you simply to speak your name and in doing so admit what has been driving you to live the life you live. God might even surprise you with an impromptu wrestling match of some sort that will take you from a "wannabe" to a person who actually lives from truth, truth that has taken root in your inner being. As soon as Jacob admitted who he was, God changed his name to *Israel*—"one who struggles or strives with God." What a strange name. How would you like that on a "My name is…" sticker at a dinner party? "Hello, my name is *I Struggle With God*." Could it be that the pursuit of our True Self requires us to struggle and strive after God? Could it be that in our constant wrestling with the Divine Other, the True Self emerges? Could it also be that in our refusal to wrestle with God, we become more and more comfortable and entrenched in the False Self?

Just who is this False Self anyway? Simon Tugwell said that when we are confused about our identity "we either flee our own reality or manufacture a false self which is mostly admirable...and superficially happy. We hide what we know or feel ourselves to be (which we assume to be unacceptable and unlovable) behind some kind of appearance which we hope will be more pleasing."[5]   Forgive the illustration, but this is the spiritual equivalent of a girdle or some other form of tight fitting undergarment that masks the bulges and ripples that we think are repulsive to everyone else. The truth is, no one cares or even sees your "love handles" because they're too concerned about covering up their own. It seems as though we are more concerned with covering up the Real Self with the False Self instead of exposing the Real Self to the transformative power and presence of Christ which in turn allows the True Self to emerge.

I'll never forget as a child going trick-or-treating on my street— Rebecca Drive. There was one house we always tried to avoid until the last stop. The lady of the house—Mrs. Hoogenboom—would always do something we dreaded. And we hated it. We could never just get our candy and leave. She always invited us all the way into her house. She would talk to us, compliment us on our costumes, ask us how old we were, and then the dreaded request: *Okay, children, take off your masks and let me see who you are*. We would reluctantly lift our masks to the sheer delight of Mrs. Hoogenboom.

I have a confession to make. I fear that God will pull a *Mrs. Hoogenboom* on me. If we're honest with ourselves, when we venture into God's presence, we're tempted to just get our candy and leave. We just want our worship fix, our 30-minute self-help sermon, our anonymous identity at church, our tax-deductible receipt, our 3-minute devotional reading, our verse for the day, and our don't-get-too-deep relationships—and then we want to leave. We fear God's dreaded request: *Okay, My children, take off your masks and let Me see who you really are.* You see, the False Self can very well be religious. We plaster on what makes us look acceptable to the religious or ecclesiastical communities to which we belong, but it only serves as a veneer to cover up the real thoughts and feelings in our spiritual core. We think that the Fake Religious Self is better than the Real Messy Self. You see, Mrs. Hoogenboom wasn't trying to be difficult. She actually wanted to be part of our lives. She wanted to *delight* in who were under the masks.

Delight?

Yes, delight! Do you remember what Tugwell said? He said that most often we assume ourselves "to be unacceptable and unlovable." Perhaps that's what you heard as a child from your parents. Maybe the relational or romantic rejection you've felt through your life has caused you to feel unacceptable and unlovable. Maybe the wounds came from a boss, a teacher, a pastor, or a total stranger whose own dysfunction splattered onto you. Therefore, you don a False Self that you deem more acceptable and more pleasing to those around you who are just as confused as you are about which "self" they are. The False Self often grows out of personal insecurities from seeds that were planted by others or statements falsely assumed by us to be true.

As a college student's recent Facebook status update eerily admits: "All we can do is fake being someone other people actually want to hang out with." Referencing Thomas Merton, Henri Nouwen in his book *The Way of the Heart* says that "the false self is the self that is fabricated...by social compulsions."[6] He goes on to say that the word "*compulsive* is indeed the best adjective for the false self."[7]   The need to be accepted socially, romantically, in the work environment, and even within our spiritual communities, leads us to obsessive, neurotic, and downright irrational behavior, all for the sake of human approval. What constitutes our acceptance from God (His prevenient love and grace) doesn't enter the story of our lives. The False Self is consumed, albeit subtly and creatively (and sometimes just out-and-out obnoxiously), with how he or she looks to a societal network that's doing the exact same thing to impress everyone else!

How much of an epidemic is this? When we meet someone for the first time, who are we really meeting—their True Self or False Self? When we present ourselves to others for the first time, who do we introduce— our True Self or False Self? How much does our personality play into this? Is our personality an accurate representation of how God wired us or is it an elaborate cover-up of which we are completely unaware? Have we lived in the False Self for so long that we actually think that's who we really are? Is the False Self simply a defense mechanism against getting hurt by those who are equally disoriented about themselves?

If you can't tell, I'm very passionate about this. Can you see how the False Self sends out countless relational ripples? The ripple effect of just one person living securely in the False Self is staggering. Marriages, friendships, ministry partnerships, employer/employee relationships, extended familial connections—all of these relationships can be carried out in the midst of being outwardly happy and hiding behind a fake exterior which we hope will be more satisfying to those around us. If just one person living this way has astronomical consequences, just imagine the ripples from a whole family, or a whole company, or a whole church that refuses to slay the False Self.

The two faces of desperation

For years I signed letters and e-mails with phrases that contained the word *desperate: desperate for Him, desperate to enjoy the moment, desperate doesn't even come close, just plain desperate, desperate but watching the lilies and the birds, still desperate, desperate but full, desperate for the Wooing, desperate for it to feel like spring, and more desperate than ever,* just to name a few. The common synonyms for *desperate*—hopeless, frantic, anxious, worried, distracted—are not accurate definitions for the spiritual context in which I use this word. For me, being desperate means that I am dissatisfied with my present condition which creates a deep yearning and longing for God's presence.

Humanly speaking, desperation (the state of being frantic and hopeless) can drive us over the Cliffs of Insanity or it can catapult us to God's heart. It can send us into deep despair or it can stir longing and desire for Jesus. Desperation can speed up our lives into even more activity and noise, or it can slow us down into silence and solitude. Being desperate either reinforces your need to be in control, or it forces you to be utterly dependent on God. Desperation can lead to sin or holiness.

I believe everyone at some level is desperate, or at least should be. Without some level of desperation we'll find ourselves slogging in resignation—resigning ourselves to a life that is far from the full life that Jesus came to give. Certain questions haunt me. In which direction does desperation have me running? To what or whom am I abandoning myself? By what means am I changing my present condition? With what or whom am I satisfying the deep longings of my soul? Who or what is my comforter?

Desperation has two faces. One face—the True Self—yearns for what can be, anticipating spiritual union with the Lover of your soul, courageously struggling to live your identity as the Beloved. The other face of desperation looks slick but empty, polished but lifeless, perhaps with a guilty tinge of knowing that you've abandoned yourself to the lesser gods of your small story. This type of desperation often wears a mask to hide the inner tumult. This is the False Self in all of his or her glory.

The True Self is "the new self, which is being renewed...in the image if its Creator" (Colossians 3:10). It's the part of us that emerges, most always painstakingly, out of the old cast of pretense into the light of truthfulness.

It's the part of us that fights off the urge to create a slick but superficial self-image and allows ourselves to struggle our way out of the cocoon in order to be transformed and "renewed…in the image of [our] Creator." We are "to put off [the] old self, which is being corrupted by its deceitful desires" (Ephesians 4:22), and we are "to be made new in the attitude of [our] minds; and to put on the new self, created to be like God in true righteousness and holiness" (Ephesians 4:23-24). *Renewed in the image of our Creator? Created to be like God?*

Just when you thought the Christian life was all about being nice and going to church, or finally getting your theology straight, or sponsoring a child in a third-world country (all good things), now we're told that our True Self (the new self) is the self that strives and struggles to robe itself in the very righteousness and holiness of God. This is a far deeper quest than many of us signed up for. We think to ourselves, *Well, I certainly don't want to be a False Self, but do I really want to be a New-True Self? Why can't I just be an Everyday Run-of-the-Mill Self?* I'll tell you why; because Jesus did not die for you to be an Everyday Run-of-the-Mill Self. Jesus did not die for the life that many of us live. He did not courageously battle against the forces of evil that day on Golgotha for us to live shallow, wishy-washy, safe lives. He fought the world of evil, so that *we* can fight the world of evil; so that we can put off the old self with its deceitful desire; so that we can live a full life (John 10:10).

Perhaps even now the first thin layer of your False Self is being gently, but painfully, stripped away. When your soul is unmasked it actually allows you to breathe deep spiritually. I remember being somewhat relieved when I lifted my Halloween mask for Mrs. Hoogenboom. I felt suffocated with it on. All I could smell was rubber and it would often get extremely humid under there. Although I was apprehensive about taking it off, I could finally take a deep breath of fresh air.

This is all so counterintuitive, isn't it? It's hard to believe that there was no shame in our original exposure and nakedness. "The man and his wife were both naked, and they felt no shame" (Genesis 2:25). This was God's original intention. We can barely even imagine that this was possible. However, the pain and consequence of their subsequent betrayal of God made clothing a necessity. In a way that I do not fully understand, sin marred the original beauty of the human body and left it vulnerable. Something so innocent and beautiful was now open to assault and lust and danger. In order to *hide*, *Adam and Eve* covered their bodies. In order to *protect*, *God* covered their bodies. Now, don't misunderstand me, I do believe clothing is a necessity! However, my question is this: have we taken this to an unhealthy extreme when it comes to our soul? When we are ashamed of our Real Self, we create and hide behind a False Self. Yet this False Self also covers up the True Self, and prevents it from ever breaking free. When this happens, the enemy of our soul laughs with adolescent glee.

Dare we make the journey that is implied in Hosea 12:2-3? "The LORD has a charge to bring against Judah; he will punish Jacob according to his ways and repay him according to his deeds. In the womb he grasped his brother's heel; as a man he struggled with God." We *need* to make the journey that takes us from manipulating others with our False Self, albeit subtly and subconsciously, to finding God and struggling with Him from our Real Self. Then our True Self can emerge—even if he or she emerges with a limp that is a constant memory of God's painful, but gracious, touch.

This is all so counterintuitive, isn't it?

Whose kingdom is this, anyway?

Jesus said, "But seek first [God's] kingdom and his righteousness, and all these things will be given to you as well" (Matthew 6:33). Whether we know it or not, when we find God we've also stumbled into His Kingdom. The King and the Kingdom are inseparable. We cannot enjoy a life of intimacy with the King and ignore the environment of the Kingdom.

The reality, though, is that we've failed to live in the certainty of Matthew 6:33. We've dabbled in it and made resolutions about it, but many have stopped short of actually living in the reality of it. I wonder why my own heart at times is pulled away from seeking first God's Kingdom, from living with a passion toward God, from truly living as a genuine citizen in the Kingdom of God. I wonder why my default setting often points me in the direction of the anxiety and complexity of my life and my own little kingdom.

G.K. Chesterton wisely observed how many Christians think: "The Christian ideal has not been tried and found wanting. It has been found difficult; and left untried."[8] That's why many of us do not live in the reality of the Kingdom of God. We've "played" Kingdom like children play house—when it gets boring and we've had one too many run-ins with the kids or the wife, we hang it up and go play something else.

In a very simple way, Dallas Willard in his book *The Divine Conspiracy* defines what God's Kingdom is: God's Kingdom is "where what he wants done is done."[9] Let that settle in for just a moment. Now answer this question: What *does* He want done and *who* is going to do it?

Jesus answered this question very plainly in the company of only eleven individuals called his disciples or apprentices. He said, "All authority in heaven and on earth has been given to me. Therefore, go and make disciples of all nations, baptizing them in the name of the Father and of the Son and of the Holy Spirit, and teaching them to obey everything I have commanded you. And surely I am with you always, to the very end of the age" (Matthew 28:19-20). So, what does He want done? Very simply, He wants disciples made and He wants us to do it. If we are seeking first God's Kingdom, we will make sure that "what he wants done is done."

There's a rather large obstacle to that getting accomplished, though. It's called "My kingdom." I'll use myself as an example, but you could very well insert your name here: *Jamie's kingdom is "where what Jamie wants done is done."* In this scenario I'm the king and what I want done you will do. This is where I believe our lives get terribly complex and complicated. Life gets rather difficult when these two kingdoms clash and when mine, at least temporarily, comes out on top—where what I want done is done instead of what God wants done is done.

Several years ago when we lived in Michigan I worked in the Special Education Department of a charter school. One particular year I worked with a special-needs kindergarten student with Down's Syndrome. Mrs. Baker was the teacher and everyone knew that she was the Queen of the Kindergarten Kingdom. I remember one day during snack time we were eating slices of bread sprinkled with cinnamon and sugar. Mrs. Baker quickly noticed that some were not eating their crust. She got everyone's attention and said sweetly but authoritatively, "My dear children, at Paramount Charter Academy we eat our crust." And with eyes as big as saucers I reached down, grabbed my crust, and shoved it in my mouth!   Mrs. Baker was simply saying, *This is what we do in my kingdom*. Out of love and respect for her, there was not a single crust left in that room.

That's the sense we need to have as citizens of God's Kingdom. Out of deep love, respect, and gratitude for the One who has all authority in our lives, we must die to ourselves. We must put to death the False Self. Why? Because the king (or queen) of my kingdom *is* the False Self. He or she reigns with great power and implements what I want. He or she *must* die.

But as Chesterton said, seeking first God's Kingdom and living out the Christian ideal is not easy. This is hard, not just because our external lives are complex, but because our inner lives are often in shambles as well. There tends to be extra baggage on the inside that we could definitely live without. Many individuals have an intricate mix of emotions, past experiences, wounds, convictions, ideas, and thoughts that keep us from doing what God wants done. The False Self is extremely high maintenance which allows little time for others.

Track with me as I connect some Scriptural dots. In Psalm 51:6 David tells us the one thing that God wants in our inner beings: "Surely you desire *truth* in the inner parts" (emphasis mine). The inner parts or the inner being is where we live from. Proverbs 4:23 says that "above all else, guard your heart, for it is the wellspring of life." Our life springs from or wells up from our heart. Therefore, we will live from whatever is *in* our hearts. In fact, *we presently live from what is presently in our hearts.* If I could spend a day observing you without you knowing it, then I would have a good indication of what is in your heart. How? Because this spring that is called life has its origins in (or springs from) the heart, the inner being.

Do you see now why God wants truth in our inner being? Do you understand why He doesn't want bitterness, defensiveness, fear, pride, a grudge, lust, apathy, revenge, anger, your past, distrust, worry, cynicism, pain, betrayal, abuse, lies, anxiety, prejudice, inferiority, superiority, a lack of identity, insecurity, greed, jealousy, hatred, rejection, perfectionism, criticism, or addiction? You fill in the blank.

All these different issues can be grouped into one of two categories: self-interest or self-preservation, both manifestations of the False Self. Total self-interest is sin. Here are a few examples: If I have pride lodged in my heart I will care more about me than God's Kingdom. If you have lust wedged deep in your inner being, you will be concerned more about your little kingdom than pursuing righteousness first. Perhaps your prejudiced heart keeps you from showing compassion to anyone that looks different than you.

Self-preservation is basically a defense mechanism and may be connected to another person's sin which has affected you. You may be an angry or withdrawn person because of past abuse in your life. You may lack identity because of someone's rejection of you. You may live in constant bitterness because you've been betrayed. Or it very well may not be a sin but something that the Enemy has used to attack you. Perhaps it's the sense of inferiority or insecurity that just dogs you. Maybe it's some type of anxiety that haunts you every day. In any of these cases, whether it's your fault, someone else's fault, or nobody's fault, would you admit that at least one of these hurts, habits, or hang-ups is haunting and complicating your inner world? Would you also be willing to admit that your life is an expression of what is in your heart?

The teaching of Jesus is clear in Matthew 12:35: "The good man brings good things out of the good stored up in him, and the evil man brings evil things out of the evil stored up in him." Our inner worlds need to be cleaned out and simplified. Would you agree? There needs to be some extraction taking place, an introspective look into the attic of our hearts, and in some cases a deep inner healing.

This may be a scary proposition, but I have some good news. God cares so much about your heart, that He will help you come to these realizations of the complexity, chaos, and reality of what's going on inside. No amount of "doing better," therapy, prescribed medication, or self-determination will bring the deep healing that many of us need. These things are not wrong, they are just woefully insufficient. We need more. We need something other-worldly. We need something supernatural. We need someone who really knows us and really knows what he's doing. We need Jesus, the One who was "sent...to bind up the broken-hearted" (Isaiah 61:1).

In Isaiah 61 and Luke 4 we are told why Jesus came. It's the essence of the Gospel. He came to bind up the broken-hearted, proclaim freedom for captives, release prisoners from darkness, and release the oppressed. Perhaps your inner being can be described in those terms—broken-hearted, captive, dark, and oppressed. The great news is that Jesus came to heal and set us free from all those inner complexities.

We need to speak our own name as Jacob finally did; to come to God as we *are*, not as we *were*, or even as we *want to be*; to stop tripping up others and allow ourselves to struggle with God. The False Self will live in self-denial of our current condition. The True Self is the honest self, the desperate self whose inner being is rooted firmly in truth. We must be willing to be spiritually transformed to the point where God, perhaps after a wrestling match, bestows a new identity and calls us to live fully and unashamedly in His Kingdom.

[1] Jamieson-Fausset-Brown Bible Commentary, http://jfb.biblecommenter.com/jeremiah/17.htm

[2] Frederick Buechner, *The Magnificent Defeat* (New York: HarperCollins, 1985), p. 18.

[3] R. Paul Stevens, *Living the Story* (Grand Rapids, MI: Wm. B. Eerdmans Publishing Company, 2003), p. 54.

[4] George MacDonald, *The Book of Strife in the Form of The Diary of an Old Soul* (London: Longmans, Green & Company, 1885), p. 207.

[5] Simon Tugwell, *The Beatitudes: Soundings in Christian Tradition* (Springfield, IL: Templegate Publishers, 1980), p. 130.

[6] Henri J. M. Nouwen, *The Way of the Heart* (New York: The Seabury Press, 1981), p. 10.

[7] Ibid.

[8] Gilbert Keith Chesterton, *What's Wrong With the World* (New York: Dodd, Mead and Company, 1912), p. 48.

[9] Dallas Willard, *The Divine Conspiracy* (New York: HarperCollins, 1997), p. 25.

3

A quick Internet search of the phrase "to live is" reveals many possibilities:

> To live is to fly.
> To live is to love.
> To live is to be prey.
> To live is to die.
> To live is a gift.
> To live is better than to die.
> To live is to change.
> To live is to hide.
> To live is to give.
> To live is a masterpiece.
> "To live is so startling it leaves little time for anything else" (Emily Dickinson).

Here is a brief English grammar lesson. "To live" is what's known grammatically as an infinitive—the word "to" followed by the simple form of a verb. Seven of the eleven examples just given include an infinitive after the phrase "to live is." Perhaps if you were to finish the phrase you would naturally include an infinitive as well.

Many, many years ago I memorized a statement that includes the phrase "to live is." But it doesn't follow this natural grammatical tendency that I just explained. In fact, the author of the phrase went with an entirely different bent when he said, *"For to me, to live is Christ."* This statement is found in the book of Philippians in the New Testament and was uttered and written by Paul the apostle who was in prison at the time.

He could have written, "To me, to live is to get out of this stinking, rotten jail," or "To me, to live is to spread the good news of Jesus," or "To me, to live is to travel and start new churches." All those options would have been true and they include infinitives which indicate some type of action. We mistakenly think that to live means to do something. Living from the True Self is not about designing a "spiritual action plan" and then performing to the best of your ability. Paul said and wrote something far different. He defined living as a Person. He did not use an adjective—to live is wonderful or painful. He did not use an inanimate object—to live is a masterpiece. No, he used a person. That just doesn't sound right. "To me, to live is...*Joe*"?

I did not do myself any favors when I memorized this verse in a grammatically incorrect fashion. I memorized it in a cadence that really confused its meaning. I didn't pause after *for to me*. I didn't stop and think what life or living really was to me. Unfortunately, when I memorized Scripture as a kid, I did it because I was forced to or because I was bribed to. (I'd memorize anything for that Hershey's bar.) Therefore, I tended to memorize Scripture verses in a static, bland, monotone manner. I broke up this verse and accented the wrong syllables, and it made absolutely no sense. Consequently I never really wrestled with what it meant or with how Paul could have painstakingly, over a long period of time, wrestled with himself and God on how to finish that phrase. I picture him stopping and pondering *how* to finish that phrase. *For to me, to live is....*

Literally, the phrase means "to...have life."[1] *For me, to have life is.... For me, to experience real life is.... For me, to really be alive is....* That is really one of the deepest desires of the human heart and the True Self. Maybe you have never verbally expressed it, but it is my guess that at least once in your life you have admitted that your life feels like an empty shell, that you feel more spiritually and emotionally dead than alive. Perhaps your heart is in a comatose state and nothing you've tried really awakens it like you desire.

Listen closely to the late 19th century Irish author, Oscar Wilde, who publicly confessed what many of us have secretly resigned to in our hearts, "To live is the rarest thing in the world. Most people exist, that is all."[2] Be honest. He nailed it, didn't he?

For many there is nothing *transcendent* in life, nothing awe-inspiring, nothing that moves our inner being. We are stuck in a physical, temporal world with the bizarre expectations of other people dictating how our life is lived. We have no idea what the writer of Proverbs meant by "the well-spring of life" because we constantly feel empty and dry. We are not living life; life is living us.

Oscar Wilde spoke as if this is just how it is, as if nothing can be done about it. In direct contrast to that, Saint Irenaeus spoke these words over 1,800 years ago: "The glory of God is man fully alive." He didn't just pull this from thin air. Jesus said, "I have come that they may have life, and have it to the full" (John 10:10). Spiros Zodhiates describes life "to the full" as a life that is "indwelt by God *but not necessarily favored by circumstances*"[3] (emphasis mine). Surely Paul was "not necessarily favored by circumstances," yet when he pondered how to craft a phrase that would define real living, he could only think of one Person. No adjective would do, no infinitive would fit the bill for what he had experienced at such a deep level. Go ahead. Say it out loud to yourself. *To me, to live is....* No Bible scholar, theologian, pastor, friend, or author can answer for you.

Kathleen Norris tells this story in her book *The Cloister Walk*: "A monk in his early thirties once told me that he'd come to the monastery not realizing what a shock it would be to suddenly not have to compete for the things that young men are conditioned to compete for in American society —in his words, 'a good salary, a cool car, and a pretty girlfriend. When all of that was suddenly gone,' he said, 'and held of no account, I felt as if my whole life were a lie. It took me years to find out who God wanted me to be.'"[4]

Perhaps we struggle with what real life is because we've held too many substitutes for life too close for too long. *To live is to have a good salary. To live is to have a cool car. To live is to have the hottest looking girl or guy in tow.* How about these? To *live is to be a member of a growing church. To live is to maintain my reputation as a good Christian. To live is to be the best husband, wife, mother, or father I can be.* Stop! Be still and silent. Take all those things away for a moment. In your mind and heart spend five minutes in monastic mode, in simple monkish existence. No salary, no car, no lover, no growing church, no reputation to uphold, and no status as husband, wife, mother, or father. Just you, standing there in a long and flowing brown-hooded habit! What is life to you now? When all is gone, does the light of God's love descend into those vacant places? And if it does, is that enough? Better yet, when the paycheck does come every week, when the car is in the driveway, when you are in relationship with another, when you are a member of a growing church, when you have maintained your personal integrity, and when you are a spouse or a parent, does the intensity of Divine Love pierce through all those things and penetrate your soul? If not, you may need to prepare yourself for some detachment.

These things must pale in comparison to the One and Only. We have been deceived by things, even innocent things. They have subtly played tricks on us and we've started defining life with a list of inanimate objects and ego-inflating actions. We must begin to see ourselves as John Eagan's spiritual director encouraged him to see himself: "one radically loved by God."[5] This is where the True Self begins to blossom and flourish. As Jesus said so tenderly to Martha, "Only one thing is needed" (Luke 10:42).

The brokenness of a king

The Old Testament calls King David a man after God's own heart. But there was a time in his life when his heart wandered. He killed one of his most loyal soldiers, Uriah, the husband of the woman (Bathsheba) with whom he had had an affair. Before we get into this part of his story, I must tell you this: *Your heart demands a life.* Your heart's very nature is to want to experience life. Why? Because, as Proverbs 4:23 says, it is the "wellspring of life." If you do not give it the life it was made for—a life with God—then your heart *will find* a little life of its own off to the side, a life that will stroke your False Self into existence. Your heart was created to connect with God's heart, but if it doesn't it *will find* something or someone else to connect with. Your heart will find some little adventure, some person that shows it attention, some hobby that seems completely innocent but eats away time and money. Perhaps your heart will find temporary relief in some addiction, significance in some job, or pleasure in some secret life. Maybe it will settle into an attitude of self pity that isolates it, or a constant feeling of insecurity that makes it co-dependent on others around you. Your heart *is* finding a way to live whether you realize it or not.

That's exactly what David's heart did. It went sniffing for life wherever it could find it because he was not giving it the life that it needed.

Now, that actually may be the answer you've been searching for. A light bulb may be going off at this very moment: *Is that why I do what I do?* Ask yourself, "Why *am* I addicted to that? Why *am* I so driven? Why *am* I such a control freak? Why *am* I attracted to that other person? Why *am* I bitter and angry?" Is it just because you're a bad person? Is it because you just can't get your act together? No, in part it's due to the fact that you're starving your heart from the full life that Jesus came to give and now it's willing to accept any life that comes along—anything that arouses the *feeling* of life—even if it's a quick-fix, shallow, and ultimately destructive life.

For a while the proverbial skeleton had been tucked safely and quietly away in David's closet. No one suspected anything except for perhaps a few trusted servants who probably knew what was going on, but dared not say anything to the king. Everyone thought that what they saw on the surface was true—that David had taken compassion on the widow of Uriah, brought her to be his wife, and had a child with her.

Then Nathan walked in. Nathan was a prophet from the Lord. I'm sure David respected the spiritual authority of Nathan, and in some respects

David probably realized that Nathan outranked him. Prophets were God's mouthpiece, and they stepped forward when the people were unwilling to hear God directly. David was most likely in that mode. He was used to conversing directly with God, but we have no record of that happening during this time period. There seemed to be a wall around David's heart that needed to be penetrated. So God supernaturally informed Nathan about what was going on. Nathan did not come into the palace like a bull in a china shop and start railing on David. Rarely is anyone talked away from the edge by a screaming lunatic. Here's the account from 2 Samuel 12:

> The LORD sent Nathan to David. When he came to him, he said, "There were two men in a certain town, one rich and the other poor. The rich man had a very large number of sheep and cattle, but the poor man had nothing except one little ewe lamb he had bought. He raised it, and it grew up with him and his children. It shared his food, drank from his cup and even slept in his arms. It was like a daughter to him. Now a traveler came to the rich man, but the rich man refrained from taking one of his own sheep or cattle to prepare a meal for the traveler who had come to him. Instead, he took the ewe lamb that belonged to the poor man and prepared it for the one who had come to him." (2 Samuel 12:1-4)

Have you ever had an experience with someone whose heart is so detached that you have to find a connecting point first before you start addressing specific issues? That's what was going on here. Nathan played this out beautifully, and with extreme tenderness told a story about a little ewe. The story took David back to a time, a time of innocence and adventure that he experienced when he was a shepherd for his father's flock, sitting in the open field with a little lamb on his lap and writing what we now know as Psalm 23.

David, do you feel that? Do you remember those days when you defended little lambs from the claws of a bear? Do you feel that love and connection? And David, how does it make you feel to know that a wealthy but arrogant man has ripped that little ewe out of the arms of the poor man to feed his own guests?

"David burned with anger against the man and said to Nathan, 'As surely as the LORD lives, the man who did this deserves to die! He must pay for that lamb four times over, because he did such a thing and had no pity'" (2 Samuel 12:5-6).

It's good to see David passionate about something, isn't it? It had been a while since anyone had seen any emotion, or any sense of justice flowing from David. It's good to see him riled up about something. It's good to see a little *life*. But it's not the life we're looking for quite yet. We've never seen David lash out with such harshness. You see, the law doesn't say anything about the death penalty for someone stealing a lamb. There's an interesting human dynamic taking place here that is common to all of us: we become especially indignant against the sins of others when we're guilty and unwilling to break that same sin. We create a diversion. *Look at them! Isn't that awful?*

Nathan's approach was to shock David's heart back into some type of semi-normal rhythm by seeing whether or not he could get a reaction that resembled David's True Self, the one we all know and love. As you can tell by David's response, he didn't have a clue why Nathan was there. As far as he knew Nathan needed a little help on how to deal with a rich guy who stole a lamb from a poor man. Over time the tiny cracks in David's heart had been widening; his heart was hardening to the point of deterioration, to the point where big chunks of his heart were falling away and becoming disconnected from what truly brings life.

Psalm 32 gives us a glimpse into what was going on. Looking back on this time in his life, David said, "When I kept silent, my bones wasted away…my strength was sapped." For quite some time he lived in silent denial, unwilling to admit that his actions had affected anyone else. Even his physical stamina (or lack thereof) told him that this was not the life of intimacy with God.

Nathan then delivered the punch line: "Then Nathan said to David, 'You are the man!'" (2 Samuel 12:7). *David, you are the rich and arrogant man who ripped a woman away from the loving arms of her husband to feed the guest of your own selfish appetite. David, you are the one who had no regard for the law or justice as you suavely wrote a note that ordered the death of one of your closest comrades.* Nathan continues to speak for God and lists everything that God has given David: deliverance from Saul, the kingdom of Israel, and (don't ask me why on this one) more wives than he knew what to do with. God even said, "And if all this had been too little, I would have given you even more." In other words, *David, I'll give you whatever it takes for you to find real life. Just don't go find it on your own. That's when things get dangerously out of hand. That's when the False Self goes from being the Poser to being the Villain.*

God proceeded to list a number of horrendous consequences that David would face throughout the remainder of his life. The son Bathsheba bore would die; other men would sleep with David's wives, and his family would never experience peace and harmony again.

"I have sinned against the LORD," David responded. The words of George MacDonald from *Diary of an Old Soul* come to mind:

> Lord, I have fallen again—a human clod!
> Selfish I was, and heedless to offend;
> Stood on my rights. Thy own child would not send
> Away his shreds of nothing for the whole God!
> Wretched, to Thee who savest, low I bend:
> Give me the power to let my rag-rights go
> In the great wind that from Thy gulf doth blow.[6]

The True Self begins to emerge from the ashes of the False Self. David finally stopped pointing fingers, making excuses, blaming others, hiding behind a mask, and living a false life. To admit your guilt is like opening a fresh wound to the care of a doctor. Pain momentarily increases as real healing starts to take place.

Before those words were fully out of David's mouth, God was graciously responding through Nathan. Nathan replied, "The LORD has taken away your sin. You are not going to die." David would no longer be eaten alive by what had been going on inside of him for the past year. Those bones that were wasting away in Psalm 32 would be strong again. The strength that was sapped would be restored.

In 2 Samuel 12 we hear David's words, but in Psalm 51 we hear his heart—a heart that was truly broken—for a heart must first be broken before it can be restored. Perhaps just a short while after Nathan's confrontation, David went to a private place and sobbed his eyes out, cried out to God, and penned some of the most beautiful words ever born from personal tragedy, words that give hope to all of us who have bowed to the lesser gods. These words communicate that although God almost never steps into the consequences, He still accepts and loves us based on His mercy, unfailing love, and compassion. God is drawn to our brokenness. He is willing to enter the chaos we have brought upon ourselves.

Have mercy on me, O God,
according to your unfailing love;
according to your great compassion
blot out my transgressions.
Wash away all my iniquity
and cleanse me from my sin.

For I know my transgressions,
and my sin is always before me.
Against you, you only, have I sinned
and done what is evil in your sight;
so you are right in your verdict
and justified when you judge.

Create in me a pure heart, O God,
and renew a steadfast spirit within me.
Do not cast me from your presence
or take your Holy Spirit from me.
Restore to me the joy of your salvation
and grant me a willing spirit, to sustain me.

(Psalm 51:1-4, 10-12)

The familiar children's story comes to mind: "Humpty Dumpty sat on a wall; Humpty Dumpty had a great fall; all the king's horses and all the king's men couldn't put Humpty together again." It's true; they couldn't fix him. Hence, someone has actually suggested that instead of the king's horses and the king's men, the King himself should have come. I have good news for you—He has! Jesus, the healer of broken hearts, is the King of kings, and He has come to bind up the brokenhearted. No matter how you fell off the wall, He's here to put you back together again.

My Nathan

In 1997 I had a Nathan in my life. He looked a lot like my wife! We were away for a romantic weekend at the Amway Grand Hotel in Grand Rapids, Michigan. It didn't take long, however, for me to figure out that this wasn't going to be very romantic. I don't think we were in the room fifteen minutes before Julie started asking me some very difficult and painful questions. In her defense, she didn't plan on throwing a wrench into the weekend. She just had some things on her mind and began expressing them. Julie's heart was more alive than mine at that time and she simply started asking questions that would begin to awaken mine. She asked questions, not about a sexual affair, but about a passionless affair with a spirituality of duty and obligation, apathy, and the status quo. Questions about our neighbors and if we cared whether or not they knew Jesus. Questions that revolved around why we were seemingly okay with doing church in such a way that produced little, if any, spiritual fruit.

Questions about my heart, and why she really didn't see much life, passion, vulnerability, or spiritual leadership. Questions and observations that felt very confrontational, not necessarily about what I was or wasn't doing, but about who I was on the inside. She knew there was more than what we were experiencing. The first layer of my False Self was being ripped off and it was painful. Of course, at the time, I had no idea what was happening. I just knew something was being dislodged inside me.

Unveiling the True Self has little to do with us, and everything to do with God. We admit that we live from the False Self by allowing our hearts to be broken and by being willing to "throw off everything that hinders and the sin that so easily entangles" (Hebrews 12:1). Obedience is one of the first crucial steps to living fully in the True Self. In fact, genuine intimacy with God depends on our willingness to obey. Jesus said in John 14:15, "If you love me, you will obey what I command."

As I think back to that time, Julie was attempting to remove the False Self and get to the real me that she knew was in there somewhere. Now, don't misunderstand, my False Self was a nice guy, a good little pastor, provider for my family, and keeper of the rules—a person who made only small, insignificant waves for the Kingdom. I was the poster child for the religious False Self, but that's not what God is looking for. He's looking for men and women who will passionately chase after His heart and stop looking for life in every dark nook and cranny they can find.

After those prodding questions from my wife, I sat in silence for a very long time. A *very* long time! Julie constantly asked what I was thinking and I found it impossible to respond. I felt like I had just been wounded, and I had. Knowing that the "wounds of a friend can be trusted" (Proverbs 27:6), I had to eventually respond in some way. The words that finally came out were ones I had never spoken before. You see, we'd had this discussion before, only those previous talks were not as deep or intense. In those instances, I had said that I would try harder, do better. And I would...for awhile. But only my outward appearance changed, and as we all know, that is not what God is looking for. He's looking at the heart and that had not yet changed.

Here's what I said to Julie this time: "Honey, I really have no idea exactly who you want me to be. I don't know exactly what you're describing and what this other reality looks like. But one thing is for sure, I'm done trying. If what you're describing is real, I have no idea how to get there or live there. I'm done. I'm done trying to do it better and work harder. If this is going to happen, it's going to have to be God's initiative." (And all of heaven gasped in silent wonder.) Needless to say, that was all God needed. He started almost immediately. He's been romancing my heart ever since like nothing else or no one else can. George MacDonald said it best:

> With every morn my life afresh must break
>
> The Crust of self, gathered about me fresh;
>
> That thy wind-spirit may rush in and shake
>
> The darkness out of me, and rend the mesh
>
> The spider-devils spin out of the flesh
>
> Eager to net the soul before it wake,
>
> That it may slumberous lie, and listen to the snake.[7]

The "crust of self" is another accurate description of the False Self. The False Self gets entangled in these webs spun to offer us pseudo-life. However, the True Self allows the wind of the Spirit to refresh and renew us and offer what we really crave—real, full life. The God who indwells us is the beginning and end of what it means to really live.

For me, to live is Christ. How about you?

[1] Spiros Zodhiates, editor, *The Complete Word Study Dictionary: New Testament* (Iowa Falls, IA: World Bible Publishers, 1992), p. 697.

[2] Oscar Wilde, *The Soul of Man Under Socialism and Selected Critical Prose* (1891. Reprint. London: Penguin Books, 2001), p. 133.

[3] Spiros Zodhiates, editor, *The Complete Word Study Dictionary: New Testament* (Iowa Falls, IA: World Bible Publishers, 1992), p. 704.

[4] Kathleen Norris, *The Cloister Walk* (New York: Riverhead Books, 1996), p. 295.

[5] John Eagan, *A Traveler Toward the Dawn* (Chicago: Loyola University Press, 1990), p. 150.

[6] George MacDonald, *The Book of Strife in the Form of The Diary of an Old Soul* (London: Longmans, Green & Company, 1885), p. 37.

[7] Ibid, p. 207.

The Grand Decrescendo

4

I was shocked to find this in the Bible:

O LORD, the God who saves me,
    day and night I cry out before you.
May my prayer come before you;
    turn your ear to my cry.
For my soul is full of trouble
    and my life draws near the grave.
I am counted among those who go down to the pit;
    I am like a man without strength.
I am set apart with the dead,
    like the slain who lie in the grave,
    whom you remember no more,
    who are cut off from your care.
You have put me in the lowest pit,
    in the darkest depths.
Your wrath lies heavily upon me;
    you have overwhelmed me with all your waves.
    Selah

You have taken from me my closest friends
    and have made me repulsive to them.
I am confined and cannot escape;
    my eyes are dim with grief.
I call to you, O LORD, every day;
    I spread out my hands to you.
Do you show your wonders to the dead?
    Do those who are dead rise up and praise you?
    Selah

Is your love declared in the grave,
    your faithfulness in Destruction?
Are your wonders known in the place of darkness,
    or your righteous deeds in the land of oblivion?
But I cry to you for help, O LORD;
    in the morning my prayer comes before you.
Why, O LORD, do you reject me
    and hide your face from me?
From my youth I have been afflicted and close to death;
    I have suffered your terrors and am in despair.
Your wrath has swept over me;
    your terrors have destroyed me.
All day long they surround me like a flood;
    they have completely engulfed me.
You have taken my companions and loved ones from me;
    the darkness is my closest friend.
    (Psalm 88)

(Be honest. Did you read this psalm? Please don't skip it. Its spirit is the basis for this chapter. Caught you, didn't I?)

One of the reasons I was shocked to find Psalm 88 in the Bible is because I didn't know we were allowed to talk that way. In *The Cloister Walk* Kathleen Norris gives a key insight into the psalms: "To your surprise, you find that the psalms do not deny your true feelings but allow you to reflect on them, right in front of God and everyone."[1]

To be quite honest, we do the exact opposite most of the time. Fig leaves were the first garment of the False Self, and we Christians have become especially adept at sewing them together to hide our real condition. When it comes to reflecting our true condition, as Norris put it, "right in front of God and everyone," we often freeze up and resort to the safety of concealment. Whether our true condition stems from our own poor decisions and actions, or those of others, or just the reality of life, we feel the need to make everything look better than it is. We offer a stiff smile and a hypocritical "I'm fine" and hope our friends can't see through it. (According to a friend of mine, the word *fine* is an acrostic for Frenzied, Incapable, Neurotic, and Exhausted. If this is true, then I'm *fine* most of the time.) Church buildings are filled with individuals who think they've got to pull it all together for an hour on Sunday morning, outwardly and inwardly, so they can worship God with all the others who obviously have life figured out. The result is that we end up offering God pseudo-praise from a well-groomed False Self.

We are unclear regarding the specific circumstances of Heman, the author of this psalm. He could have had a physical or mental or relational condition, some illness or issue that had him talking like this. Whatever the case, it obviously reached an emotional and spiritual level, at which point he had to take it up with God. Perhaps he meant to be non-specific so that his words could filter into the myriad of human situations that require such expressions.

Have you ever found yourself in a similar circumstance, knowing that God *is* the one who saves you, but simultaneously having the darkness of human reality mingle with that truth? Have you ever wondered if it's acceptable to feel both extremes at the same time? *God, You are the one who saves me, but my soul is full of trouble; I am cut off from Your care. You've taken my closest friends from me, and not only that, they don't like me anymore. God, if You're supposed to save me, why do You reject me and run and hide from me? Why are You so angry with me? Why is darkness my closest friend?*

We've been led to believe that our journey with God is solely a linear path in which we move in and out of good days (when God is around) and bad days (when He's not around). We assume the bad days (when God is not around) should be experienced as quickly as possible, so we can get to those good days (when He is around). We equate "good days" with "God is near" and "bad days" with "God is nowhere to be found." We encourage each other to get through those bad days so we can experience Jesus again.

But here's the paradox, the contradiction to our human reasoning: "Even though I walk through the valley of the shadow of death,...*you are with me"* (Psalm 23, emphasis mine). Here is a further irony: On the good days, when God is supposed to be near, we seem to forget all about Him, as if He's not even around. Could it be possible that those days of lament that seem never ending are actually the "God is near" days? Could we dare believe that though the darkness may hide God's form, it actually exposes His true presence? F.B. Meyer tackled this incongruity in his book *The Way Into the Holiest*:

> With too many of us the inner life is variable and fickle. Sometimes we have days of deep religious earnestness, when it seems impossible for us to spend too long a time in prayer and fellowship with God. The air is so clear that we can see across the waters of the dividing sea, to the very outlines of the heavenly coasts. But a very little will mar our peace, and bring a veil of mist over our souls, to enwrap us perhaps for long weeks. Fall on your knees and grow there. There is no burden of the spirit but is lighter by kneeling under it. Prayer means not always talking to Him, but waiting before Him till the dust settles and the stream runs clear.[2]

The False Self, however, often goes into protection mode. There are two lines of defense as we attempt to stay safe, as we try to secure ourselves, as we try to protect our hearts from harmful influences from without and from within. There's everything *we can do*, and there's everything *God can do*.

We can secure our airports and beef up Homeland Security; we can hire security guards and buy security systems, and we can hold our security blanket. We can buy insurance, we can hide our money in our mattress, and we can stay close to home and never go anywhere. We can limit our relational depth and our spiritual vulnerability.

We can do all those things, but something funny happens when our own line of personal security gets breached. When something penetrates our line of defense, *we automatically question if God is there, if He loves us, if*

He's for us. We tend to think *Why did God not do something to stop all that?* Then we start to feel insecure because we think God is holding out on us. We begin to feel as though we are not "good enough" to meet the challenges of life. We become overwhelmed by a feeling of helplessness in the face of problems. We start believing that we are inadequate or incompetent. We begin to feel the sense of being unaccepted, disapproved, or rejected. All because we've equated two things that should *never* get equated with each other: We think that *God's Love equals the state of having no problems,* which can only lead to the logical conclusion that on bad days God hates us.

Before you categorically deny that you're guilty of that, just think back for a moment. Have you ever said or thought anything like this: *God, why are You doing this to me? What did I do to deserve this? I thought we had an agreement. I'll straighten up and fly right in exchange for a pretty painless life.* Or do you notice how we respond on a warm, sunny spring day? *God, thank You for Your blessings and love. What a wonderful day!* Then, when a freak spring snowstorm hits, or the dark clouds and pelting rain ruin our plans, we wake up, scowl, and wonder why God is making life miserable.

C.S. Lewis, in his book *The Problem of Pain,* discusses what we're to do with pain since it *is* a reality of life. He said that a common human perspective is that "we want...not so much a Father in Heaven as a grandfather in heaven—a senile benevolence...whose plan for the universe [is] simply that it might be truly said at the end of each day, 'a good day was had by all.'"[3]

I have a confession to make. Secretly, I wish that were true. I wish that at the end of every day I could say that "a good day was had by all." *God, why can't I just have an endless string of good days? That would prove Your love for me, wouldn't it?*

Most of us know—at least with our intellect—that God loves us. It sure *feels* like it as long as the pain and problems of life stay on the other side of our line of defense, on the other side of the security fence that we set up to protect ourselves. But as soon as the problems penetrate our lines of defense, we tend to fall apart. We question God's love and reel in insecurity. We begin to self loathe.

What if life is not like that at all? What if that is a total illusion? What if that is a tactic of the Enemy? I believe the reality is something more like this: There are two lines of defense, two security fences. We'll always have ours. As long as we're breathing we're going to try to secure ourselves. It's perfectly acceptable and advisable to have home owner's insurance and I'm glad we go through security check-points at airports. But one thing is certain, and I'm sure you already know this: *our defenses are not impenetrable.* Problems and pain penetrate our defenses; they breach our security.

But we have a second line of defense—the cross of Jesus Christ that symbolizes and communicates His unconditional, radical love. The love that Jesus demonstrated on the cross has the power to provide security beyond anything built or provided by human hands. It has the force to withstand any earthly or supernatural opponent.

In Romans 8:35 the apostle Paul asks an important question. It's the same question that we ask secretly in our own dark night of the soul. It's a question of God's goodness and His heart toward us. It's a question that asks what God is really made of, if He will surely come through for us. The question is this: "Who shall separate us from the love of Christ?" *God, I feel like something might get through. I feel like someone might actually put me right over the edge to the point where I can't sense Your love.*

Paul continues, "Shall trouble or hardship or persecution or famine or nakedness or danger or sword?" Shall trouble? Will this crush, this press, this external squeeze—will this separate me? Will hardship? Will this anguish, discomfort, and internal depression—will this sever me from Your love? Will persecution? Will this relentless pursuit of the enemy against my heart—will this, Lord, separate me from Your love?

Shall famine? Will physical hunger or this extreme spiritual emptiness I feel—will this break up our relationship? Will nakedness? Will the condition and sight of my physical body make You turn away in disgust? Shall danger? If I become the innocent victim of a random shooting, Lord, would that separate us? Will the sword? Lord, if I were to die for my faith and become a martyr, would You still be there for me? Will any of these things separate me from You and Your love?

"No, in all these things we are more than conquerors through him who loved us. For I am convinced that neither death nor life, neither angels nor demons, neither the present nor the future, nor any powers, neither height nor depth, nor anything else in all creation, will be able to separate us from the love of God that is in Christ Jesus our Lord" (Romans 8:37-39).

Will natural death separate me? No. Will anything in this life, this physical existence sever me from You, Lord? No. Will angels, those celestial soldiers superior to man in whose presence human beings drop to their knees—will angels separate me? No. Will demons, those unseen evil beings whom we war against—will they disconnect me from You, God? No. Will powers, will anyone's ability to control me—will that separate us? No!

Will the present, will anything near at hand, the here and now, what's happening right now, these bad days—will my present circumstances split us up? No. What about the future? The unknown, those possibilities or probabilities to come down the road, what we hope for or fear? Will the known or unknown future separate us? No!

Will height, will everything that's so hard for me to understand, everything that's over my head—will that get in the way and wiggle it's way in between us, Jesus? No. What about depth? Sometimes I feel like I'm drowning. Will you let me drown, Lord? No. Will anything in the entire created universe separate me from You, Lord? No, nothing! God will not walk out on you. Henry Blackaby, who wrote the book *Experiencing God*, told this story:

> When our only daughter was sixteen, the doctors told us she had cancer. We had to take her through chemotherapy and radiation. We suffered with Carrie as we watched her experience the sickness that goes along with the treatments. Some people face such an experience by blaming God or questioning why He doesn't love them anymore.

At times I went before God in prayer, and I saw behind my daughter the cross of Jesus Christ. I said, "Father, don't ever let me look at circumstances and question Your love for me. Your love for me was settled on the cross."[4]

God does not demonstrate His love for us by giving us good days. No, "God demonstrates his love for us in this: While we were still sinners, Christ died for us" (Romans 5:8). Good days do not prove His love, and bad days do not separate us from His love. God said, "See, I have engraved you on the palms of my hands" (Isaiah 49:16). The Lord said, "Never will I leave you; never will I forsake you" (Hebrews 13:5). Jesus said, "And surely I am with you always, to the very end of the age" (Matthew 28:20).

Back to Heman and Psalm 88: his heart's ache is the Grand Decrescendo. He begins with some hope and a little volume, but then his mood quickly descends and gets bleaker and more depressing with every phrase until there is nothing but a whisper in utter darkness. We're fighting for our brother to pull the nose up before he crashes and burns, to start praising God at the end like all the other psalmists. We figure he must have flunked out of Psalm Writing School! And to top it off, this is the only psalm this poor bloke wrote.

Heman certainly isn't clothed in his False Self. There's no slick and polished facade. If you were to ask him, *"Hey, Heman, how ya doin', buddy?"* you'd probably get an earful. My guess is that most of us secretly wonder if we have permission to be disturbed, to this extent, in our soul in the presence of God and others. If we believe God cannot handle our muddled and messy sincerity, we have rendered God Almighty incapable of handling anything less than perfection; therefore, we live in a constant state of spiritual dysfunction. We conclude that this God of ours, as nice as He is, cannot meet us where we are.

The German theologian, Ernst Wilhelm Hengstenberg said, "The darkness is thickest at the end just as it is in the morning, right before the rising of the sun."[5] Heman somehow found God and his True Self in his utter darkness even *before* the sun rises. You see, the True Self is not the Perfect Self. The True Self is very often the Desperate Self in naked vulnerability before the Lord. Whether we like it or not, the True Self is frequently unveiled by the kind of suffering that makes God seem far away.

Living in the Grand Decrescendo means living in that thick darkness, the time between times, not demanding that the sun rise, but waiting for the sun to rise, however long it takes. To be honest, I don't like this any more than you do. Time stops or at least seems to. Desperation becomes our closest friend. The sun refuses to peek over the horizon of our inner world. We're told that good things come to those who wait, but waiting, especially with no timeframe, can become so maddening that we start to feel like God's latest rejection. We're battered and bruised by wave after wave of what seems like God's wrath. Terror grips our core. We feel like we're drowning, going under, giving up. We lie back and let the raging flood sweep us away. The dark side of desperation defines us and overwhelms us. No amount of psycho-babble can pull us out. No prescription medication can turn the tide. Spiritual advice seems like pablum. And there is not a church program on the planet that is sufficient to rescue us from the whirlpool of despair.

Heman's soul-mate, Job, comes to mind. According to scholars Job is the oldest book in the Bible. It was written even before Moses wrote the first five books of the Old Testament. This is significant because what made Job famous, so to speak, were the circumstances in his life that were beyond his control. It's noteworthy that the oldest writings in the Scriptures tell a story about *life beyond our control*; circumstances that force a detachment from everything we *thought* we needed to make life work. This is an old thread that weaves its way through the history of humankind—an irresistible loosening of our grip on life; an ancient story of losing life to find it. We must believe that in this time of detachment *God is on the move*. Even though we may *feel* like He has forgotten us, *nothing* can separate us from His love.

Over 500 years ago St. John of the Cross called this experience of detachment "the dark night of the soul." The dark night of the soul is far more than a bad day, insufficient funds in the bank account, your favorite team losing the championship (the Pittsburgh Steelers in Super Bowl XLV), a fight with your spouse, the stock market taking a dip, or seasonal depression. Susan Muto, in her book *John of the Cross for Today: The Dark Night*, describes it this way: "The night in question throws a veil over one's ability to understand what is happening. One has no choice but to proceed in faith. Memories of what used to be fade…. All one can do is inch forward on filaments of hope."[6]

Perhaps the reason that I've rarely heard the story of Job taught in church settings, or Heman's psalm for that matter, is that it does not really provide the answers we're looking for. If we're honest, when we're in our own dark night, we search for answers to the "why" and "now what" questions. But neither Job nor Heman cleanly answer either question. These questions are a normal human response to suffering…*but we can't stay there.* It's probable that we may never get the "why" and "what now" questions answered, so we must "inch forward on filaments of hope."

Interestingly enough, this is not a bad place to be. Heman and Job describe the utter rawness of the human soul when it meets up with circumstances beyond our control; when our emotions are wrung dry; when friends betray us; when we lose everything that gave us an identity; when we lose our voice of influence; when we try to praise God but mutter words that sound like gibberish; and when we spit and sputter trying to reconcile the truth of God's salvific presence with the undeniable gut-wrenching pain of our life's circumstances. According to Henri Nouwen it's just as significant to feel God's apparent absence as it is to feel His real presence. To feel God's perceived absence indicates that the heart is sensitive to the Divine Void. Woe to the person who has no clue or feeling as to whether God is here or there.

Thank you, Heman, for breaking our silence and shattering the phari-saical mask of our False Self. Sometimes darkness *is* our closest friend, a friend that escorts us from the world of glitter and pretense into the inner regions of aloneness, pain, and truth; a place where Christ will be formed in us perhaps to a greater degree than if we lived a life free from heartache. Better to find God and our True Self in the middle of a dark night of the soul than maintain our False Self in the midst of a well manicured, but counterfeit, life.

---

[1] Kathleen Norris, *The Cloister Walk* (New York: Riverhead Books, 1996), p. 92.

[2] Frederick Brotherton Meyer, *The Way Into the Holiest* (New York: Fleming H. Revell Company, 1893), p. 262.

[3] Clives Staples Lewis, *The Problem of Pain* (1940. Reprint. New York: HarperCollins, 2001), p. 31.

[4] Henry Blackaby and Claude King, *Experiencing God* (Nashville: B&H Publishing Group, 2008), p. 19.

[5] Ernst Wilhelm Hengstenberg, *Commentary on the Psalms: Volume 3* (Edinburgh: T&T Clark, 1848), p. 98.

[6] Susan Muto, *John of the Cross for Today: The Dark Night* (Notre Dame, IN: Ave Maria Press, 1994), p. 21.

5

Desperation can bury you deeper in the muck and mire of your own myopic existence or it can awaken the spiritual recesses of your heart that you never knew were there. There is a mysterious occurrence that happens to your heart when desperation drives you to God. During this process of spiritual awakening (and yes, it *is* a process), there seems to be a time when a person crosses a baffling threshold where his or her relationship with God goes from explainable to inexplicable, from reasonable to unreasonable, from sensible to foolish. I've listened to those who wax eloquent on theological issues, and then I've experienced a few close friends who have been ravished by God's love and simply shake their heads without commentary. I'm unimpressed and untouched by the former, but brought to tears by the latter.

Perhaps in your desperation you have meandered into that mystical realm and know exactly what I'm talking about. You have discovered your inner mystic that sees and experiences more of God than just the parts that make sense or fit into theological outlines; these glimpses wed the supernatural God and the human heart.

During the summers of 2004 and 2010, I was able to spend some time in Alaska; there I experienced several activities that are not normally on my daily agenda: drinking in the splendor of a breaching hump back whale, hiking numerous trails, wading and kayaking in glacier-fed lakes, clamming, seeing moose meander through the neighborhood like they owned the place, camping at the foot of snow-capped mountains, and watching salmon force their way against the strong current of the Russian River. And the mountains simply oozed majesty and mystery. My sister and brother-in-law, who live in Alaska, are master hikers, so I was especially intrigued one day when they suggested that they would lead a hike "above tree line." Now, that's not a phrase I use often. *Good-bye honey, I'll see you for supper. I'm going above tree line.* "Tree line" is that line of demarcation where almost all trees, shrubs, and grasses do not exist. It's just too steep and too rocky. My response to this hike above tree line was *Really, we can do that? I can really go there, and without an oxygen tank?*

The world above tree line is a completely different world. One that I never knew existed. A place I literally did not want to leave. We spotted a black bear bounding up and over the ridge. We drank water (filtered, of course) from the streams flowing from the mountain lakes fed by the melting snow. The interior of the mountain range engulfed us. I felt like I was in the palm of a gigantic hand. It was clean and untouched by human mechanisms. No power lines, no billboards, no asphalt, no industrial noises, no rude drivers, just God's creation at His very best. I felt like an honorary member of the von Trapp family! There was no explanation for what we were seeing and experiencing other than...*God*.

We didn't go all the way to the top of the mountain, but we did hike up to the "saddle," which is a high point that connects two mountains. As we got on top of the saddle and looked through to the other valley, we realized we were looking down at snow! My brother-in-law asked if anyone wanted to go for a ride. *Go for a ride?* Now, mind you, we didn't have anything to *ride on*, except what God has equipped all of us with. So, off we slid on our backsides down a snow shoot in 75 degree weather. It was exhilarating!

We then went back to the saddle and just hung out. My brother-in-law mentioned that we'd stay there and rest for a while, and told us to tell him when we were ready to hike out. That was the wrong thing to say because no one wanted to leave. We rested there in silence, soaking up the sun, filling our lungs with unpolluted air, and letting the wind lap our faces. After about 20 minutes my brother-in-law said, "Well, we've got about a four-mile hike out of here; maybe we should get going." Nobody moved.

The question I asked myself earlier still echoes in my mind: *We can do that? We can really go there? I thought observing from a distance was as good as it got.* I was wrong.

The same mental paralysis happens in our minds toward God. We observe God from a distance and think to ourselves, although we seldom admit it, that where we are at this moment is as far as we can go. We mistakenly believe that spiritual formation has its limits. Our heart asks if it is really possible to start a trek to the interior of God's heart. If we believe the lie that we can't, then our distance from God will create a distortion of Him. As with any object, the further away it is, the smaller it appears. Perhaps we even convince ourselves to keep a safe distance from God so as to not disturb the slumbering Deity or interrupt the pseudo-stillness of our lives. Realistically, though, finding God involves going farther and deeper than what we think is possible. It's being invited into the deep end after years of splashing around in the shallow end with our floaties on.

Many individuals remain unable to move closer to God's heart because the limitations of their own human intellect keep them paralyzed. One's intellect alone is simply unable to find God. When we seek God with our *hearts* is when we find Him, Jeremiah said. This contrast reminds me of the first Lamaze class my wife and I attended many years ago. The instructor had never given birth to a baby, yet she waxed eloquent on pain and pain management, proper breathing, and what it was like to experience child birth. It's difficult to really believe someone who is merely offering verbal descriptions from a book with no real life experiences to give any real meaning to the information. I'm not suggesting that our personal spiritual experiences trump truth; however, when spiritual concepts never become spiritual realities, the desperation of the heart may just start seeking other avenues for fulfillment. I've seen it happen, and it's tragic. I've rubbed shoulders with those who think God is the sum total of what they know intellectually about Him, and they're not impressed. Their desperation (longing, desire), like water cut off from one route, finds another path to travel.

My mind returns to November 1997 when I was sure that weekend away with my wife would meet my dreamy, romantic expectations. (Remember the story from chapter three?) She turned to me and expressed her doubt, dissatisfaction, and lack of expectations of what God could really do, as well as our inability and lack of desire to be involved in the radical things God is capable of. Needless to say, that brought an abrupt end to *any* romantic expectations, let alone *dreamy* ones. I was shocked speechless that she dared to think that of her pastor-husband. *I'm a good little pastor,* I thought. *What else does she want?* It may have been the end of romance for the weekend, but it was the beginning of my desperation and my spiritual trek above tree line. And now, I can't thank my wife enough for ruining our weekend.

The truth is, until God started shaking up my nice, neat little world, I had no idea who He was. I had a proper theological understanding of Him according to my denominational bent, of course. However, my acute awareness of Him was completely absent. When my awareness did kick in, He was nothing like I had understood Him to be. My heart had been co-matose for a long time, totally unresponsive to the solely cognitive attempts to understand Him and know Him. Could it be that an acute awareness of God should be one of the most essential desires of the human heart? Could it be that cultivating a sensitive heart, a perceptive consciousness of God, is more important than displaying our intellectual prowess about Him?

Understanding and knowing are two different species. The Scriptures are clear that a complete cognitive, intellectual understanding of the Almighty—what He does and why He does what He does—is impossible. "My thoughts are not your thoughts, neither are your ways my ways," God said (Isaiah 55:8). He goes on to say that His ways are higher than our ways and His thoughts higher than ours (Isaiah 55:9). However, *knowing* Him is different. Jesus prayed an agonizing and weighty prayer in John 17 that we would *know* His Father. On our behalf He prayed, "Now this is eternal life: that they may know you, the only true God, and Jesus Christ, whom you have sent." Eternal life is not strictly an immeasurable amount of time; it is a qualitative relationship that Jesus wants us to experience now. Many choose to *understand* God because, in a sense, it's easier. It's easier to systematize God into formulas and definitions than to explore, experience, and get to *know* His very heart.

In truly knowing God, we will be satisfied in Him. St. Augustine said, "Our hearts are restless until they find rest in Thee."[1] This goes right to the heart of the matter. To those of us who've found our deep soul's satisfaction in God, we simply bow our heads in reverent agreement. We've sensed the haunting restlessness and experienced the indescribable satisfaction. We are the answers to the prayer of Jesus. It *is* possible to experience a qualitative relationship with God that takes us above tree line, past those who find it easier to learn about the mountain in the classroom than take the exhausting but exhilarating journey to a place they've never been.

With a modern intellectual backdrop setting the scene, one courageous pastor dared to be a voice crying in the wilderness. In the middle of the last century, A. W. Tozer pleaded in *The Pursuit of God*, "For it is not mere words that nourish the soul, but God Himself, and unless the hearers find God in personal experience they are not the better for having heard the truth."[2]

Personal experience and the accompanying emotions have been downplayed as shifting sand, a quite unstable approach with which to pursue a relationship with Jesus. Yet there would be an outcry if I instructed all of you who are married to begin relating to your spouse on a strictly intellectual, systematic basis. Take all emotion and personal experience out of it. Send flowers out of mere obligation. Make sex purely mechanical with no prior emotional attachment or exhilarating afterglow. I understand that emotions alone do not make a relationship; however, to block all emotion is to dismantle the image in which God created us—His image. Emotions indicate heart activity or the lack thereof. When your heart feels something, your emotions express it. When the heart of Jesus was broken, He cried at the death of His friend, and was enraged at the gall of the money-sucking mongrels in the temple. When His heart was filled with compassion, He wept over Jerusalem. When His heart was light and filled with love, He bounced children on His knee and told everyone within ear-shot to become like them if they wanted any chance of experiencing and enjoying His Kingdom. He continued the celebration by inexplicably creating the best wine from water at a Jewish wedding reception. His emotion in the Garden of Gethsemane before His death is unprecedented. The pain in His heart seeped through His very pores in bloody form. The chaos of the cross caused Him to feel forsaken, yet loved by His Father all at the same time. Jesus unapologetically *felt* His experiences.

John Wesley embodied this concept. He was in his spiritual prime during the first half of the 18th century. Spiritual activity, even missionary endeavors, provided an identity for him. He knew, taught, and preached the Scriptures. He and his brother, Charles, provided a "method" for spirituality which eventually became known as Methodism.

Enter God.

Wesley began experiencing troubling thoughts much like this one that he recorded in his journal: "I went to America to convert the Indians; but oh, who shall convert me? Who, what is he that will deliver me from this evil heart of unbelief? I have a fair summer religion. I can talk well; nay, and believe myself, while no danger is near. But let death look me in the face, and my spirit is troubled. Nor can I say, 'To die is gain'!"

Wesley wrote the following journal entry after hearing Luther's preface to Romans read aloud during a meeting: "About a quarter before nine, while he was describing the change which God works in the heart through faith in Christ, I felt my heart strangely warmed. I felt I did trust in Christ, Christ alone, for salvation; and an assurance was given me that he had taken away my sins, even mine, and saved me from the law of sin and death." The very next morning he recorded this: "The moment I awakened, 'Jesus, Master,' was in my heart and in my mouth; and I found all my strength lay in keeping my eye fixed upon him and my soul waiting on him continually."[3] Wesley's identity was no longer bound up in a life of activity and traveling; his identity was now in Christ. His heart was no longer defined solely by a method; it was now "strangely warmed."

The *warmed heart* is intriguing. It's how Wesley described the sensation of his conversion. I guess it's not unlike what happens when you have been captured by the love of another and begin to love deeply in return. In an effort to remind the church in Ephesus what it was like when they first experienced the love of Christ, the apostle John recorded in Revelation this haunting, nerve-hitting indictment: "You have forsaken your first love!" They had walked away from the innocent, mysterious, heart-palpitating love that characterized the first time true love had taken root in their hearts. A heart warmed by the unquenchable love and grace of Jesus is worth holding on to.

Many a relationship with God, however, is purely cognitive. Please understand that cognitive is not bad. We need our cognitive faculties to survive each day. We must think, retrieve information, do simple math, and use our common sense. Our cognitive ability allows us to interact with bodies of knowledge and truth, especially the Scriptures. Being *purely cognitive* toward God, however, is not spiritually healthy. Prior to November 1997, to me God was not a Person. He was an exact science that was to be studied. The hard questions of life were answered with meticulous precision. When people seemed bewildered and needed answers, I gave them the "right" answers as the cure for their confusion. Usually it was something they needed to do or not do to clean up their messy lives.

In all honesty I wasn't doing this out of pride or egotism, but simply out of ignorance, and a sorely inaccurate perception of God. I was operating from the default method of my formative years, rather than from a desperation that sent me searching. There are scores of books on my shelves of authors trying to explain God to me. They speak of His immutability, omnipotence, omnipresence, and omniscience. They touch on something about *kenosis*. There are outlines that communicate that the image of God in man is composed of intellect, emotions, and will. Another book talks about the canon being closed. And the Holy Spirit is described in ways that make indigestion more appealing.

There is a temptation to throw our intellectual arms around God instead of letting God put His loving arms around us. There's a tendency to try to figure Him out, instead of allowing His influence to mold and shape us. In all my vain cognitive and legalistic attempts to get in touch with God (my own version of the Tower of Babel), I was not stunned or transformed until God touched me.

Knowing and experiencing God at the level of relationship will not become a reality if we value understanding God on paper more than knowing Him in person. *Understanding* becomes *knowing* when your heart is engaged enough with God's to push you over a line you would have never crossed on your own.

Admit it; we're very uncomfortable when God doesn't make sense, so we make Him make sense. We create words to define the Indefinable. We construct a system to describe the Indescribable, and then wonder why God leaves us cold. If we genuinely pursued and experienced God, I believe our conclusions about Him would be less conclusive. Instead of nailing down facts about Him, we would be caught up in the Inexplicable. We would stand drop-jawed in His presence. The need to understand Him in the solely cognitive theological sense would sink beneath the weight of His Immensity.

John Eagan, author of *A Traveler Toward the Dawn*, made this poignant statement: "The contemplations I've so often made cease to be a mere exercise and become rather a reality I live and taste."[4] That is the line we must cross, the path we must travel. Those who have truly experienced

God know that there is an astronomical difference between "mere exercise" and the reality of living in and tasting His presence. It's the difference between reading the recipe for "Crawfish Curry with Mango Chutney" (or watching it made on The Food Network) and actually gathering the ingredients yourself, preparing the food, creating a fine dining atmosphere, inviting a special friend, and partaking of this fine cuisine. Here is another statement by John Eagan that has, quite honestly, rattled me: "I could spew off statistics. But it was all from books, hardly rooted in my own experience."[5]

Please understand that I am not pushing experience just for the sake of experience. Personal experience must be rooted in truth. Our personal experience of God must validate, not contradict, what the Scriptures reveal about Him. But something tells me we're afraid to experience what the Scriptures reveal about Him. Something tells me that we haven't even scratched the surface of this profound relationship, this deep and penetrating *knowing* that the sacred writings speak of. It's much safer to keep God in a box and to keep ourselves wrapped in fig leaves. Intimacy requires an unveiling, a moment when our soul is disrobed; an experience when "the king is enthralled by your beauty" (Psalm 45:11); that occasion when we "are led in with joy and gladness; [and] enter the palace of the king" (Psalm 45:15).

John Eagan's confession brings to mind the days when I lived exclusively from my head. My head was full, but my heart was empty. My mouth contained a barn full of prayers, but the words were bare. My wife admitted to me later that she had great difficulty listening to me pray from the pulpit. She could see right through my vague generalizations and empty words. The eyes of my heart held nothing but a blank stare. My heart finally accused me of starving it and eventually indicted me on charges of abandonment. I had left my heart unguarded, not knowing the real treasure that it is.

Blaise Pascal, the 17th-century French philosopher, said it this way: "It is the heart which perceives God and not the reason." We cannot find

Him or love Him without engaging our own heart. The False Self lives in fear of this engagement because the heart contains places we'd rather not go. The True Self, however, risks the journey by standing in his or her own ruins just to catch a glimpse of God.

Another mountain

Perhaps this story of an experience I had in January 2001 will somehow capture what I mean.

The winding road seemed to have no destination. The locals told my friend and me that this was the only way in and the only way out, and if we wanted a view that was up close and personal, this was the way. Earlier in the day we had a view from quite a distance and were impressed, but that wasn't enough. I felt compelled to get as close as I could. So, after downing a burger and some fries, we began the last leg of our journey.

With every curve and turn our excitement swelled. Then, without warning, she would "jump" out from behind one of her smaller counterparts and freak us out! Still, we wanted to get closer, to see for ourselves if this phenomenon was really true.

Beautiful, mysterious, captivating. As we got closer, the beauty and mystery echoed louder in my heart. We crossed one more bridge and rounded one more bend, and suddenly got the stunning view we'd been waiting for—Mt. St. Helens. At last, a view unhindered that allowed us to drink in her beauty, yet simultaneously contemplate the devastating effects of her judgment.

Helen has a reputation of blowing her top. On May 18, 1980, at 8:32 a.m., with the force of 5,000 atomic bombs, she unleashed her consuming fury and caused the largest landslide on Earth in recorded history, completely devastating the lives and landscape of the Toutle River Valley forever. Her effects were felt around the globe. She now bears the scar of the internal heat and pressure she could not contain; a cubic mile of her is gone, exposing her inner beauty.

My friend and I didn't gaze at Helen wondering what ecological ingredients came together to create such an explosion. We didn't speculate what kind of stone she was made up of. We didn't analyze the soil. We didn't spend much time reading and wandering around the exhibits. We didn't even head for the gift shop to buy cheap knick-knacks. We just gazed in disbelief. We sat and listened intently to a man who was an eye-witness to this overwhelming natural disaster. His personal experience of it brought history to life in a way that no book is capable of.

What mental picture do you paint when you see God in your mind's eye? Have you ever gotten close enough to see His inner splendor, His aching heart?

The spiritual scientific method of observation, hypothesis, and experimentation has reduced God to something less than He actually is, and we mistake our study of Him as communing with Him. The entire Bible has been reduced by some to a list of "ologies" that bring order to the inspired writings. We conclude that being baffled, even somewhat, is not good, so we attempt to bring an end to our confusion by re-organizing the Scriptures into systems our minds can handle, but leave our hearts out in the cold. We've taken unbelievable stories that reveal the very heart of God and placed an "ic" (an appropriate syllable, I must say) at the end of these heroes' names to somehow explain how God was working at that point in time. The Adam*ic*, the Abraham*ic*, and the David*ic* covenants are all relationships between God and men that now have a scholarly feel, and offer no hint of the underlying riveting story.

Consider what Jesus said to the religious pop stars of His day in John 5:39-40: "You diligently study the Scriptures because you think that by them you possess eternal life. These are the Scriptures that testify about me, yet you refuse to come to me to have life." If I could be so bold as to paraphrase Jesus: "Get your nose out of your scroll just for a moment and take a stroll in My direction. Don't worry about having everything down pat by your diligent study. Close your book and come to Me. I've got the life you've always wanted." In Oswald Chambers' words, "We are not asked to believe the Bible, but to believe the One Whom the Bible reveals."[6]

In the late 1990s God unmistakably pointed me and my family in the direction of starting a new church. After having served in several well-established churches, this new assignment was a bit overwhelming. Ministering to a post-modern culture was like pursuing an elusive concept. *Does God really know what He's doing? I don't have a church-planting degree.* And if it had not been for the God-induced euphoria that numbed us to the reality of what we were doing, we could have very well retreated. I call it a numbing, God-induced euphoria because in all of my years as a Christian and a pastor, I had never experienced God in a way I could not explain. Let me say that again: *I had never experienced God in a way I could not explain.* I could produce a litany of attributes and tons of fill-in-the-blank outlines, but all my cognitive powers could not describe what God was doing or why He was doing it. I was left shaking my head as to why God would want me to leave the secure confines of a well-established, reputable church and reach out to people in a post-modern culture. To get my nose out of the study guide and start walking in God's direction meant walking across the street in my neighbor's direction.

What will it take for us to start exploring a whole new section of the mountain that we've only seen from a distance but never experienced? What will it take for us to go to the interior of God's heart to find out that He's better than we ever could have imagined? What's that line of demarcation for you? What takes you deeper into God's heart? What needs to happen for you to begin seeing with your spiritual eyes? What will it take to release you from the cognitive corridors of your False Self and allow you to come back from the mountain just shaking your head after experiencing something that words cannot describe? What will it take to keep your mouth shut and your ears and eyes open? Are we desperate enough to venture above tree line?

John Eagan described it this way: "So in my personal history there comes the blessed moment when the Spirit seeks me out, touches me in my heart, gives me a moment where I experience this God and know that I am in his presence. My emptiness is addressed, my depths are uncovered, and desire and attraction are awakened for God. This is almost always a surprise for a human being, something unplanned, not on the radar. It is God finding me in my ordinary life....This first touch...has been renewed again and again in my life, in moments of awareness, times both gentle and intense, subtle and obvious, through both absence and presence experiences, ache and ecstasy, emptiness and fullness."[7]

Years ago a friend of mine admitted her desire for this type of an awakening toward God. She wanted me to tell her what to do, to wrap it up for her nice and neat and give it to her as a gift. *"Just tell me what to do,"* she sobbed, *"Just tell me what...."* Unfortunately, I couldn't. If the answer was as simple as one, two, three, I would have earned a fortune years ago. We've believed the delusion that as soon as we accept God's saving grace, we immediately fall from it and have to work our way back into His graces. Hence, *just tell me what to do.* We thoughtfully consider the fabrication of the Evil One that tells us we're "something" before belief in Christ and then screams that we're "nothing" after we trust Jesus. The propensity for most Christians, no matter where they are on their spiritual journey, is to boast and gloat over what they've done to maintain a state of "good graces" with God. They've got the ribbons, certificates, trophies, plaques, degrees, recognition, and pats on the back to prove it, yet their hearts are empty; the well is dry. And the misfortune is that they dare not tell a soul. They dare not dismantle the False Self for fear that others will realize their life was nothing more than a hoax. They end up stranded because they pour their energies into the Christian hustle and bustle instead of letting Christ pour Himself into them. Remember, we are *God's* "workmanship" (Ephesians 2:10), not our own. We must bare the canvas of our hearts and allow the Artist to begin His work. Yes, we are created to do good works, but not before God accomplishes His.

In direct contrast to John Eagan's witness of how God touches a heart, Frederick Buechner describes his mother in his memoir, *Telling Secrets*: "My almost entirely beautiful mother was by no means heartless, but I think hers was a heart that, who knows why, was rarely if ever touched in its deepest place. To let it be touched there was a risk that for reasons known only to her she was apparently not prepared to take."[8]

That is the tragedy of more people than I dare admit. There is a risk to being desperate. There is a risk to having Christ formed in you. To have an awakened heart and to live from your True Self means to have a vulnerable heart toward God that puts everything up for grabs, even the cognitive comforters and legalistic securities that have given us a sense of uneasy calm for so long.

---

[1] St. Augustine, *The Confessions of St. Augustine*, trans. J. G. Pilkington (Edinburgh: T. & T. Clark, 1876), p. 1.

[2] Aiden Wilson Tozer, *The Pursuit of God* (1948. Reprint. Camp Hill: Wing Spread Publishers, 1982, 1993), p. 9.

[3] John Wesley's entire journal can be viewed at http://www.ccel.org (Christian Classics Ethereal Library)

[4] John Eagan, *A Traveler Toward the Dawn* (Chicago: Loyola University Press, 1990), p. 172.

[5] Ibid, p. 36.

[6] Oswald Chambers, *My Utmost for His Highest* (London, Edinburgh: Marshall, Morgan & Scott, 1927), p. 127.

[7] John Eagan, *A Traveler Toward the Dawn* (Chicago: Loyola University Press, 1990), p. 125.

[8] Frederick Buechner, *Telling Secrets* (New York: HarperCollins Publishers, 1991), pp. 15-16.

6

An analogy

I am a boat, a small vessel being tossed hither and yon on the thin surface of a tumultuous sea. The wind batters my masts. My decking is slick and my bow heaves with every swell. The rain comes in sheets. Sometimes it's very dark, while at other times the sun's rays from a clearing in the distance allow me to navigate with the naked eye, rather than by instrumentation alone. At times my rudder seems to respond with keen precision to any variance of the wheel. Yet in other instances, it equally refuses to counter-answer the force of the wind and the buffeting of the waves; it's as if I have no rudder at all.

Over time the storm passes, but I am exhausted. I bob up and down, tired and fatigued from wrestling with nature. The gentle breeze carries me away and I'm too tired to care where. I wonder if my fate will always lie in the forces that are out of my control. In this lull it seems that all I do is gather just enough strength to battle the next storm front. Everything looks the same—endless sky and water in a kind of gray hue. How long can I keep doing this?

Something in me desires a transformation. Not into something I'm not—not an airplane or an animal or a human. I was created a vessel and a vessel I shall be. A vessel, however, that can navigate the deep instead of being sentenced to the surface. A submarine perhaps.

Yes, a vessel that can sink to the depths, not out of resignation, hopelessness, and defeat, but out of intention, out of a de-

sire to live in the calmer and deeper currents. But isn't it scary down there? There are creatures there that I've never seen on the surface of the sea. There are underwater mountains and valleys, and I wonder, with a sense of doubt and cynicism, if navigation is really any easier in the depths. Yet the Spirit of the Depths beckons me. My own soul beckons me. Dare I go to such an unknown, uncharted place? A small vessel on the surface is all I've ever been and known. Suddenly there is security in what is familiar.

I've heard that the currents in the depths are powerful and strong. Not in a defeating kind of way, but a revealing way. Currents that reveal my True Self and that anchor me in a reality much deeper and truer than the surface tension of the sea.

I take the risk and begin the journey of transformation. The deep places are not a different life, just a truer reality of the same life. I experience the actual ebb and flow of feelings instead of static numbness. I feel joy and sorrow, ecstasy and pain, humor and solemnity, acceptance and rejection, confidence and fear. I scale the heights and traverse the depths of the ocean floor rather than bobbing aimlessly. Somehow I do not fear where these underwater currents are taking me; I trust these currents in a way I never trusted the elements on the surface. There is beauty here, and yes, frightening scenes as well, but a sense of calm and peace beyond comprehension.

Maybe I've been a submarine all along just hanging out on the surface, a place that I wasn't made for and where I really didn't belong. Perhaps that is why, even with all its variety, adventure, and unknowns, the depths actually feel more like home.

The essence of spiritual formation

The struggle is to keep the soul in the depths while the other parts of yourself deal with the tension on the surface. This will be a life-long struggle. What many churches and Christians call "spiritual growth" often falls short because of a person's inability to know and navigate his or her own heart and complicated life. We're not even sure our complicated life *can* be influenced or penetrated by what most churches purport as discipleship. The fill-in-the-blanks, the "study guide in the back," the "relevant" sermons, and the "vibrant worship" just aren't enough to counteract the raging storm. I believe that discipleship as modeled by Jesus with His disciples is central to the Christian faith. We have simply wandered far from that ancient path and have settled for something far less potent.

We *must* have Christ formed in us (Galatians 4:19) in order for spiritual transformation to take place. This is a spiritual mystery that cannot be bottled or boxed into a curriculum or program. Spiritual formation involves putting yourself where you know you need to be whether you want to be there or not. In saying this I am not suggesting that mere duty constitutes our motivation to be spiritually formed. What I am saying is that sometimes we need to be coaxed or pushed, albeit gently and lovingly, into the influential flow of God's Spirit. Spiritual formation is the direct influence of God's Spirit on the redeemed human spirit and our receptivity and responsiveness to that influence. It's stepping into the stream of the Spirit and allowing the current to take you to God's heart. This lifelong process involves the mystery of what the apostle Paul said in Galatians 4:19: "I am again in the pains of childbirth *until Christ is formed in you*" (emphasis mine). Spiritual formation for the Christian is the everyday experience of having Christ formed in him or her. These experiences can be transcendent or incredibly mundane, mystical or practical, awe-inspiring or painstaking, contemplative or action-packed. It is not merely imitation of certain divine qualities or a dutiful persistence in countless "spiritual" activities. It involves the formation and growth of the Divine Other in us as we surrender our will to His and as we allow His loving embrace to comfort and calm our restless souls. Spiritual formation is not about bringing our external behaviors into conformity with some moral code. Our spirits need to be formed, not just our morals. Paul knew Christ had been *conceived* in the Galatians; now he wanted to see Him *formed* in them.

The apostle Paul said that there *are* "deep things of God" (1 Corinthians 2:10). God *has* revealed them, and the Spirit helps us search them out. Solomon said that "the purposes of a man's heart are deep waters, but a man of understanding draws them out" (Proverbs 20:5). Your heart was created to yearn for depth, and God's heart is a bottomless treasure of inexhaustible riches and yearns for a cherished relationship with you. *Seek Me*, He says, *find Me, know Me, and love Me*. That is what is meant by deep. Deep describes a quality of relationship, not vast cognitive awareness, not verse-by-verse expository preaching, and not a mastery of the original languages of Scripture. As helpful as those things may be, that is not the kind of depth I'm referring to.

Now, I realize, deep is relative. Ten feet down is deep compared to the surface, yet there is so much beneath ten feet to be explored. Whether you're at the surface, ten feet down, or more, my encouragement is to go deeper with God than where you are now. For those who constantly ask the question about what you're supposed to *do*, listen up! Enter in and enjoy Him. It is not unlike the way we develop deep relationships here on earth—it requires transparency, vulnerability, honesty, conversation, openness, the desire to please, times of leisure and relaxation, the ability to communicate well, the sensitivity of not wanting to hurt or grieve the other person, the willingness to spend dedicated time, the eagerness to be a servant and help bear burdens, and the zeal to go the extra mile. In fact, ask yourself this: what is involved in my deepest and most intimate relationships on this earth? The same is needed in your relationship with God.

When I was in junior high, I lived across the road from a pond that my friends and I affectionately named "Billy's Pond." (I have no idea why we named it that. I didn't even know a Billy.) That was our spot for adventure and discovery. My friends and I loved experiencing all angles of pond life. We fished, measured and tagged the fish, took notes on the fish we caught, threw the fish back in, and then even re-caught some of the tagged fish which we measured again to see if they had grown. We took the temperature of the water in the spring, summer, winter, and fall. We even threw old Christmas trees into the water so the smaller fish would have some protection. And we played hockey in the winter.

But one angle eluded us—we wondered what pond life was like under the surface of the water. No, we did not take up scuba diving. Our idea was more dramatic than that. We drew up plans for an underwater observatory. Our idea was to weld together three or four 55-gallon drums to create a tube that we could semi-submerge and anchor to the bottom of the pond. Our sketch included port-hole type windows that would allow us to observe pond life from beneath the surface. Our imaginations had us rowing to the center of the pond in our boat, opening up the lid to our observatory, and one at a time lowering ourselves down the tube into a different world. I wish I could tell you we actually accomplished this feat. We didn't. Our attempts to go beneath the surface of Billy's Pond got no further than our imaginations and sketches on a piece of paper.

How do we get past the surface with God? Past the small talk? Past the misunderstandings of who He really is? Past the misconceptions our shallow minds and frail hearts have erected? Past the distorted *Imago Dei* that we've created that keeps us living insipid spiritual lives? Past our own False Self? A.W. Tozer in *The Pursuit of God* asks, "With the veil removed by the rending of Jesus' flesh, with nothing on God's side to prevent us from entering, why do we tarry without? Why do we consent to abide all our days just outside the Holy of Holies and never enter at all to look at God?"[1]

A vicarious life

We all have the tendency to live life vicariously—to experience life secondhand, to journey through this life as if we were taking part in the experience or feelings of another, yet refusing to experience it ourselves. We ride the proverbial coat-tails of someone else. We tend to live out our dreams and imaginations, even our spiritual lives, through other people instead of trusting God enough to fully engage with the world around us. This is why many parents push their children to excel in areas like athletics;

if their kids can succeed where they themselves failed, their lost dreams can be recovered.

Our tendency to live vicariously is what makes reality TV so popular. We desire a little adventure or romance in our lives, but instead of pursuing it on our own, we'll live it out through someone else as we watch *The Amazing Race* or *Survivor* or *The Bachelor*. We'll take up residence on the couch with a bag of chips and a Diet Pepsi as we watch someone else doing what we wish we had the guts for.

Often in our search for God we find other things that satisfy us temporarily. Food, physical and emotional relationships, mental fantasies, good sales and a credit card, a new this or that, substance addictions, romance novels, social networking, our job—whatever it may be—can sabotage the seeking process by providing a quick fix before we get to God's heart. The Enemy strategically places camouflaged landmines in the path toward God that make Him less attractive than the immediate pleasure before us. Before long we start believing that this God is too hard to find, that plunging the depths is just too exhausting, so we abandon all efforts to push through in our search for Him.

We either live out our dreams and adventures through someone else as we sit in our La-Z-Boy, or if we do get out of our easy chair, we create an adventure of our own that is nothing but a shameful simulation of the real thing. We become spiritual sleep walkers. We're moving around, but accomplishing very little, and what we are accomplishing is actually causing our spiritual demise.

To experience something vicariously is to never really experience it. To experience the cheap imitations is to live confidently in the False Self. The greatest travesty is to live a vicarious spiritual life and never take the plunge yourself. In one of his sermons entitled "You Are Accepted," theologian Paul Tillich said, "We feel that something radical, total, and unconditioned is demanded of us; but we rebel against it, try to escape its urgency, and will not accept its promise."[2] We become immobilized at the prospect of responding to the call of the deep. We convince ourselves that we are sentenced for life to bobbing up and down on the surface. The False Self opts to stay with the familiar, even if it destroys us.

Why are we frightened to act on the internal spiritual desire we feel bubbling up from within? The answer may be similar to what I felt about our underwater observatory: it was fun to think about, but impossible to pull off—so we thought. The idea was crazy anyway. My fear of being seen as wildly passionate (or maybe foolish) about this adolescent dream, and my insecurity that I had what it took to build this contraption paralyzed me. I failed to act on desire. The classic spiritual disciplines such as prayer, silence and solitude, Scripture reading, fasting, worship, and contemplation actually give desire an outlet. In later chapters we'll discuss the role a few of these spiritual disciplines play in channeling our spiritual desire to the point where we may actually feel like we've taken the plunge into the depths. Remember, the underwater observatory was not the end; it was simply the means by which we would engage with the underwater world of Billy's Pond. Living in the depths means that we must honestly and vulnerably place ourselves in the streams of these spiritual disciplines in order to engage with and gaze upon the beauty of God.

In the opening paragraphs of *The Sacred Romance*, Brent Curtis and John Eldredge urge us with these words: "Some years into our spiritual journey, after the waves of anticipation that mark the beginning of any pilgrimage have begun to ebb into life's middle years of service and busyness, a voice speaks to us in the midst of all we are doing. *There is something missing in all of this*, it suggests. *There is something more.*"[3] Listening to that internal voice may be the invitation you need that will set your spiritual transformation into motion. God invites you to leave the surface tension of the sea in order to experience the depth you secretly desire.

---

[1] Aiden Wilson Tozer, *The Pursuit of God* (1948. Reprint. Camp Hill: Wing Spread Publishers, 1982, 1993), p. 41.

[2] Paul Tillich, *The Shaking of the Foundations* (New York: Charles Scribner's Sons, 1955), chapter 19.

[3] Brent Curtis and John Eldredge, *The Sacred Romance* (Nashville: Thomas Nelson, 1997), p. 1.

7

I'm struck by the following description of Jesus Christ in Revelation 1:8: *"…who is, and who was, and who is to come…."* To experience the true height and breadth and depth of Jesus, we must experience Him as the *was*, the *is*, and the *is to come*. To leave out any of these dimensions is to experience Jesus only partially, to never go beneath the surface or above tree line. The False Self, who refuses to engage the totality of Christ, is satisfied with a one-dimensional Savior, and thus is left with a spirituality that lacks true height, breadth, and depth. The person of Jesus and our personal spirituality cannot be separated. Spiritual formation is tied to Jesus, who is in the process of being formed in you. This Jesus who transcends time and space is the One who coaxes our True Self to the surface as He forms Himself in us.

Most of us don't have a problem with knowing the *was*-Jesus. We can rattle off in a heartbeat many different historical facts about Him. We know His miracles, His famous sayings, the sequence of the Passion Week, the gory details of His death, and the apologetic proof for the resurrection. And we *should* know these things. But it's there we get stuck. We are not only trapped in the past as it relates to clothing styles or the furniture in our living room with the protective plastic, we're also stuck with a *was*-Jesus. I understand why this is the case for many Christians, because a *was*-Jesus is very convenient. Like anything old and from the past, we get it out once in a while, converse about its past significance in our lives, and then put it back in the cedar chest or the attic and turn off the light. It's very expedient for us to get out the *was*-Jesus around Christmas and Easter because that's expected. When asked about their spiritual journey, some Christians can only comment on their initial conversion, because nothing is presently happening that would prove that Jesus is alive and working today.

Experiencing a *was*-Jesus is not only convenient, it's dangerous. It's dangerous in the sense that to only experience a *was*-Jesus is to live disconnected from any present spiritual realities. Jesus becomes nothing more than a faint memory or a character in a book. Maybe the reason that many believers are transfixed on a *was*-Jesus is because an *is*-Jesus is very difficult to comprehend. No other person is ever described this way and you really can't experience any other individual as *was*, *is*, and *is to come*.

There seems to be a strange phenomenon that occurs when someone dies. Have you ever been close to the surviving spouse or a surviving child when they've said something like, *"Oh, she may be gone, but her spirit is here"*? Or, *"I just know he can see and sense what's happening here."* Or, *"I bet she's looking down on us right now."* People are so desperate to hang on that they convince themselves that a mingling of the spirit world among the living and dead is possible. We'll believe that it's possible to hang on to someone's spirit because that belief gives us some type of security and hope. Yet as far as Jesus is concerned, He just *was*. If we can do the mental gymnastics about a dead relative who *was*, we should be able to grasp this concept with Jesus, who not only *was*, but *is*.

One of the ways we experience the *is*-Jesus is to realize that His Spirit *is* with us. In John 14 right after Jesus told His disciples of His exit plan, He said this: "I will ask the Father, and he will give you another Counselor to be with you forever—the Spirit of truth" (John 14:16-17). Introducing the *is*-Jesus! His Spirit *does* mingle with our spirit. He *does* see and *is* involved in what's happening. He *does* provide security and hope because the Spirit of Jesus *is* with us.

Jesus continues comforting His friends: "The world cannot accept him, because it neither sees him nor knows him. *But you know him, for he lives with you and will be in you*" (John 14:17, emphasis mine). And we think it's comforting if the spirit of our dead grandmother shows up every once in a while! If you're a believer, the Spirit of Jesus lives *in* you! The apostle Paul prayed in Ephesians 3:16 that "[God] may strengthen you with power through *his spirit in your inner being*" (emphasis mine). No one else can do that. Yet our rational, modern mind kicks in and tells us that's foolish. The Enemy suggests that we should just keep Jesus where He belongs: in the Bible. If we listen to our own short-sighted intellect, if we bend an ear to the whispers of the Enemy, we will be stuck with a *was*-Jesus. And that is exactly what our False Self is most comfortable with.

Be honest with yourself. You *know* if you've experienced the *is*-Jesus. It's that indefinable reality that wakes you up on the inside. It's the gentle nudge and soft whisper that awakens your slumbering soul. When it happens, you ask, "How have I missed it for so long?" But it feels uncomfortable initially. The True Self will always feel a bit ill-fitting at first. In fact, the Enemy will attempt to convince you that your True Self is really your Hypocritical Self. When you experience those mystical "above tree line" moments, when you *are* actually patient and kind and understanding, when you actually reserve time throughout the day for quiet intimate moments with God, when you stand up against some injustice, when you and your spouse have those moments when the veil is lifted—these are the times you will hear the devilish accusation that you're nothing but a hypocrite. *Stop acting like you're trying to pull it all together. We all know who you really are.* This impish voice must be silenced or it will arrest any progress in our quest to experience the *is*-Jesus.

Brennan Manning asks a series of riveting questions in his book, *A Glimpse of Jesus*: "Who is the Jesus of your journey? How would you describe the Christ who is the still point of a turning world for so many people and an irrelevancy or embarrassment to countless others?"[1] He continues, "Who is the Jesus of your own interiority? Describe the Christ that you have personally encountered on the grounds of your own self. Only a stereotypical answer can be forthcoming if we have not developed a personal relationship with Jesus."[2] Manning is not suggesting that you *define* Jesus "on the grounds of your own self" as if each of us is allowed to come up with our own specialized "Jesus" that works well within our individual ideologies and theologies. He is simply reiterating that we must not settle for textbook answers if someone were to ask what Jesus means *to you.*

Suppose you were in a small group of people talking about the *is*-Jesus. Could you relate? Could you chime in with your own personal testament of how Jesus walks and talks with you? Or would you simply nod your head wondering, *"What in the world are they talking about?"*

For so long I waved the *was*-Jesus flag and secretly wondered why no one seemed very excited. I also secretly wondered why I wasn't very excited. No one was particularly thrilled to follow because I had relegated Jesus to the past, wedged tight in the pages of Scripture, plastered hard and fast on the flannel graph, instead of allowing Him to roam free in my present realities. We must position ourselves and invite Him to the center of our present lives as the *is*-Jesus, or we will slowly suffocate under the delusion that we are responsible for our lives turning out pretty dog-gone well. If we do not begin to interact with the Spirit of Christ in us, we'll risk waking up some morning with the terrifying realization that we have gained the whole world, but sacrificed our own souls.

Who *is* Jesus, you ask? He *is* the Lover of my soul. Jesus *is* my Advocate when the Accuser rushes into His presence and says, "Do you know what Jamie just did?" Jesus *is* the Forgiver of my old heart and the Giver of my new heart. He *is* my Hero, my Rescuer; the Heart behind the passionate pursuit of my soul. Jesus *is* my friend, my divine soul-mate, the Ultimate Love of my life. He *is* the reason tears streak my face now more than any other time in my life. He *is* the motivation for getting up in the morning when the weight of life crushes me. Jesus *is* my prompter; I can sense those gentle nudges that push me toward what I should do, or pull me back from what I should not do. He *is* my constant companion; even when I am alone, I know I am not alone because Jesus *is*. He *is* my calm center in the middle of a raging storm. Jesus *is* also the one who calls me into dangerous, risky adventures that actually make life worth living.

He *is* all of that to me and more; therefore, I cannot wait for the Jesus that *is to come*! You must know the *was*-Jesus to know the *is*-Jesus. And you must intimately know the *is*-Jesus if your heart is ever going to skip a beat for the Jesus that *is to come*. For years I was more concerned about the proper sequence of events surrounding Christ's return than I was about actually anticipating Jesus Himself. Finally I stopped trying to figure out the *when* and started anticipating the *Who*.

Let me take a moment here and make perfectly clear what the center-piece of Christian spirituality is. Jesus *is* the only way to God. "The Son is the radiance of God's glory and the exact representation of his being" (Hebrews 1:3). Jesus said, "I am the way and the truth and the life. No one comes to the Father except through me" (John 14:6). We will not find God in His salvific totality if we do not express faith in who Jesus *is* and the grace He offers us. If we do not engage Jesus, we will find only snippets of God that make little sense and jeopardize our very life. The Scripture is clear: "Whoever believes in him is not condemned, but whoever does not believe stands condemned already" (John 3:18). The promises of full life and intimacy with God are for those who have "by grace…been saved through faith" (Ephesians 2:8). To those who still possess a "heart of stone" (Ezekiel 36:26), the spiritual concepts and realities that I have been describing serve only as inspirations.

Let me warn you: you will not look forward to the Jesus that *is to come* if you don't know and love the Jesus that *is*. It would be similar to your great Aunt Ruth, with whom you've had no contact for 27 years, visiting you from Paducah. There's no real relational connection, so you really aren't looking forward to her visit. From what you do remember, Aunt Ruth has a lot of weird mannerisms that you've never really taken the time to understand. And she smells funny to boot. It's like that strange dynamic at a family reunion: you're related to everyone yet you hardly know a soul, and you're supposed to be glad you're there.

When you only experience Jesus as *was*, you secretly say to yourself when you wake up at night, *"There's got to be more than this,"* but you dare not admit it to anyone for fear that they'll think you're off your spiritual rocker. Jesus said in John 10:10 that He came so that we "may have life, and have it to the full." A full life, a life above tree line, a life beneath the surface, a life that is drawn mysteriously toward the mountain, a life that embraces our True Self—this is not only knowing Jesus as *was*, but knowing Him as *is* and anticipating Him as the *is to come*.

The Spirit of Christ

The Spirit of Christ, or the Holy Spirit (also called the Holy Ghost), is the *is*-Jesus. We need to nurture this relationship if Christ is to be formed in us. Just as Jesus is "the radiance of God's glory and the exact representation of his being" (Hebrews 1:3), so the Holy Spirit exactly represents Jesus. However, something has gotten lost in translation. Many Christians view the Spirit through a distorted lens. They see Him as an old schoolmaster complete with ruler in hand just waiting for some unsuspecting student to step out of line. Or perhaps Brussels sprouts—good for you, but boy, does He leave a bad taste in your mouth. Some think that He really is a ghost. In my formative years I was told ghosts did not exist and that I wasn't to believe in them, but this one *did* exist and I should believe in this holy one. He's been represented as an unwanted house guest that just won't leave, a boring theological topic to be studied, outlined, and dissected, and the holy impetus at certain revivals that make you laugh hysterically or bark like a dog.

As we attempt to grasp the reality of the Holy Spirit, we must remember the words of A.W. Tozer: "What comes into our minds when we think about God is the most important thing about us. Were we able to extract from any man a complete answer to the question, 'What comes into your mind when you think about God?' we might predict with certainty the spiritual future of that man. For this reason the gravest question before the Church is always God Himself, and the most important fact about any man is not what he may say or do, but what he in his deep heart conceives God to be like."[3]

Perhaps an excerpt of Romans 8 from *The Message* paraphrase can help us conceive in our deep heart what God—as the Holy Spirit—is like. The apostle Paul said this to the believers in Rome:

> Those who enter into Christ's being-here-for-us no longer have to live under a continuous, low-lying black cloud. A new power is in operation. The Spirit of life in Christ, like a strong wind, has magnificently cleared the air, freeing you from a fated lifetime of brutal tyranny at the hands of sin and death…Those who think they can do it on their own end up obsessed with measuring their own spiritual muscle but never get around to exercising it in real life. Those who trust God's action in them find that God's Spirit is in them—living and breathing God!…It stands to reason, doesn't it, that if the alive-and-present God who raised Jesus from the dead moves into your life, he'll do the same thing in you that he did in Jesus, bringing you alive to himself? When God lives and breathes in you (and he does, as surely as he did in Jesus), you are delivered from that dead life. (The Message)

At best this is a fleeting possibility for most Christians, and at worst a cruel joke. *Yeah, right! You haven't lived my life. God has never come through for me.* Many believers still live under that low-lying black cloud.

Why is that? "You, dear children, are from God and…the one who is *in* you is greater than the one who is in the world" (1 John 4:4, emphasis mine). But we believe the exact opposite. We believe that the one who is in the world is stronger than the One who is in us. We live lives of quiet desperation (in the words of Thoreau) and resign ourselves to the belief that our life's bleak situation, our family hang-ups, our personal sin, and our individual disappointments have somehow come out of the ring the winner. We swallow the evening news hook, line, and sinker and believe that somehow the forces of evil in this world have won the day.

Think again. After promising His disciples that the Holy Spirit would come, Jesus said, "I have told you all these things, so that in me you may have peace. In this world you will have trouble. But take heart! I have overcome the world" (John 16:33). Jesus is realistic about life, and that's why He hasn't left us alone. Simply stated, *the Holy Spirit is the answer to our deepest needs.* Jesus said, "I will ask the Father, and he will give you another Counselor to be with you forever" (John 14:16).

The word "another" literally means "another of equal quality."[4] The original word for Counselor means "to comfort, encourage or exhort."[5] Spiro Zodhiates comments that "He undertakes Christ's office in the world while Christ is not in the world as the God-Man in bodily form."[6] The word is also translated "Comforter," "Advocate," and "Defender." All of these descriptions are the answers to some of life's biggest struggles, to our soul's deepest needs. The Holy Spirit—the *is*-Jesus—simply continues to do what He has seen the Father and the Son doing all along.

The Holy Spirit is "Counselor," meeting our need to be counseled, to be guided in this life, to be given wise advice, to be mentored, to have someone to talk to, to have someone who will genuinely listen. The issue is not our refusal to accept counsel or guidance or advice; we accept these things all the time. The issue is where and who we get our counsel from. It's probably not the smartest thing to get counseling from a new car salesman on whether or not to buy a new car. He will tell you yes! It's probably not the brightest move to get counseling from a loan officer on whether or not you can afford that new car. He will find a way to tell you that you *can* afford that new car!

Our tendency is to succumb to every signpost along the way that tells us where we need to be heading. Every credit card application that comes in the mail is an attempt to guide you and counsel you. *You need this for your financial security*. Every billboard, every advertisement is an attempt to counsel and guide you. The problem is that we ask *ourselves* if we think it's a good idea! We forget the message of Proverbs 3:5 so quickly: "do not lean on your own understanding." The False Self leans heavily on his or her own understanding. The True Self, on the other hand, simply asks the Spirit of Christ who dwells in him or her if this or that is a good idea. But why don't we do that? *We don't do that because we don't expect an answer.* Most of us don't really believe that we'll get an answer. Perhaps I'm ludicrous enough to believe that because He called Himself a Counselor, His desire is to counsel us. God impresses upon us internally the right way to go, and through His Word gives us direction. There's another reason we don't ask: *we don't want the answer.* This simple yet profound activity of asking God is synonymous with walking in the Spirit, and I believe it will radically transform our lives. Asking the Spirit to counsel us on the purchases we make would change our spending habits and cripple our economy. Asking God how and where we spend our time would revolutionize our schedules. Asking the Counselor about our eating habits would actually make us healthier. Asking the Spirit about how to navigate relationships would actually do wonders for the health of those relationships. Life is far too complicated to navigate without a counselor, and the Holy Spirit desires to fill that role for us, calling Himself by that name.

Next, the Holy Spirit is "Comforter," meeting our need to be comforted, to be reassured, to be calmed, to be at peace. Why? We need comfort because of this reality: in this world you will have trouble. Comfort is needed in times of grief; reassurance in times of uncertainty; calm in times of stress; and peace in times of conflict.

The Spirit's embrace and comfort is mysterious and supernatural. It is God meeting you at the end of your rope and reassuring you at your greatest hour of need. The True Self allows this to happen. The False Self chases other comforters. There are many other things in this life that we head toward to soothe the wound, to numb the pain, to deaden the ache of a life full of trouble. We do it all the time—a spending spree that we cannot afford, a little too much Southern Comfort than what's good for you, an unhealthy romantic relationship, living life on the couch in front of the TV, throwing ourselves into our job to get away from the pain at home, busyness, an affair, food, sleep, religious legalism, isolation, and co-dependency. These are all "comforters" to which we become addicted, and they only mask the pain temporarily.

It's interesting that a common name for a blanket or bedspread is *comforter*. A comforter is designed to cover you, to keep you snug and secure in its environment. It's the same with the Holy Spirit. The Comforter is here to cover you, to bind up your broken heart, to heal your wounds, to wrap Himself around you and provide security. And best of all, He's not temporary. He will "be with you forever" (John 14:16).

Next, the Holy Spirit is an "Advocate" and "Defender," meeting our need to be believed in, to be defended. The term *advocate* indicates some-one stepping between you and something or someone else in order to benefit you.

Several years ago we purchased a laptop computer from an electronics store in our area. In less than a month, it "blue-screened." We took it back to the store and they "fixed" it, but then it blue-screened a second time. I immediately took it back and let the customer service representative know that we had purchased the Cadillac of warranties which included a new computer if anything drastically happened to it over the course of 4 years. So I said, "Here, I want a new computer." To which he replied, "Oh, we can't do that." I responded politely, "I believe the salesman told me that if anything happened to this computer that made it nonfunctional I was to bring it back and I'd get a new computer." To which he replied, "Yes, but we have nothing to do with that. You have to go through..." and he named the big corporate computer giant's name. Now with a slight tone of sarcasm, I said, "You can't be serious." He handed me a 1-800 number, and I departed the store a much less happy camper than when I walked in. Why? When I walked in I thought I was going to have an advocate. I thought I was stepping into a safe place and that I was going to hear, "Of course, sir, we're on it. We sold you this computer. We'll take care of this for you." What I got was *You're on your own. Have fun taking on the computer giant all by yourself.*

The eighth chapter of the book of Romans describes the miraculous way in which the Spirit steps in as our Advocate. "The Spirit helps in our weakness. We do not know what we ought to pray for, but the Spirit himself intercedes [steps in] for us with groans that words cannot express" (Romans 8:26). Have you ever been in that spot where the words for any type of audible prayer escape you? Have you ever been in that place where you don't even know what to think or feel regarding any type of communication with God? It's as if you are numb and speechless. In those moments the Spirit is doing what He does best and what you need most. He is communicating to the Father on your behalf. He is being your Advocate. He is stepping in and doing something you are unable to do. Many times I have simply prayed four words: *Spirit, do Your thing.* And when He does, He interprets our silence with "groans" that cannot be translated into any human language. One theologian said that "these groanings represent what might be called inter-trinitarian communication, divine articulations by the Holy Spirit to the Father."[7]   The Spirit steps in on our behalf and does what we cannot do.

The Spirit not only steps in between us and God, He also steps in between us and the Enemy. Revelation 12:10 describes the devil as "the accuser of our brothers who accuses them before our God day and night." Before you enter into a relationship with God through faith in Christ, Satan thinks you are a pretty good person. After you become a believer, his tune changes. *You're an absolute wreck and disgrace. You don't belong in God's family. Look at you! Jesus gave His life for you?* It's into this scenario the apostle John shouts, "My dear children, I write this to you so that you will not sin. But if anybody does sin, we have one who speaks to the Father in our defense—Jesus Christ, the Righteous One. He is the atoning sacrifice for our sins, and not only for ours but also for the sins of the whole world" (1 John 2:1-2). The Holy Spirit, who is "another of equal quality" is the One who comes alongside us as our Advocate and steps between us and the Enemy in the form of our Defender. He speaks in our defense. The Spirit stands between us and the heckling of the Enemy and says, "Back off, he's mine, she's mine." Although we are not perfect, He believes in us. The literal sense of 1 John 1:1-2 is that of a defense attorney, not a prosecutor. He's not out for a conviction. The Spirit is not out to prove us guilty. He is out to prove us forgiven, loved, accepted, and adopted.

Do you see that the continuous, low-lying black cloud has been magnificently cleared by the strong wind of the Spirit? Do you see that we have been freed from a fated lifetime of brutal tyranny at the hands of sin and death? Do you see that walking in the Spirit and living in the Spirit is not something to be dreaded, but something to be embraced? The Spirit of Christ is active on our behalf, counseling, comforting, and defending. The *is*-Jesus is the answer to our deepest needs. This is what our True Self craves.

---

[1] Brennan Manning, *A Glimpse of Jesus* (New York: HarperCollins, 2003), p. 24.

[2] Ibid, p. 25.

[3] Aiden Wilson Tozer, *The Knowledge of the Holy* (New York: HarperCollins, 1961), p. 1.

[4] Spiros Zodhiates, editor, *The Complete Word Study Dictionary: New Testament* (Iowa Falls, IA: World Bible Publishers, 1992), p. 1107.

[5] Ibid.

[6] Ibid.

[7] John MacArthur, *The MacArthur New Testament Commentary: Romans 1-8* (Chicago: Moody Publishers, 1991), p. 467.

8

Several years ago I read the following words from the Old Testament:

> Can plunder be taken from warriors, or captives rescued from the fierce? But this is what the LORD says: "Yes, captives will be taken from warriors, and plunder retrieved from the fierce; I will contend with those who contend with you, and your children I will save. I will make their oppressors eat their own flesh; they will be drunk on their own blood, as with wine. Then all mankind will know that I, the LORD, am your Savior, your Redeemer, the Mighty One of Jacob." (Isaiah 49:24-26)

Throughout that day I deeply pondered those words, but then I took it a step further. I cranked up *The Gladiator Waltz* from *The Gladiator* sound track. I closed my eyes and imagined. Then I spoke the words out loud as the music swelled. I literally got chills. Anyone walking past my office at that moment probably thought, as Brennan Manning so aptly describes, that the cheese was sliding off my cracker!

After my return to reality from the blood-drenched battlefield, I walked away with this thought branded on my heart: *To know that my God will defend me like that makes my heart soar. My God is for me! If God is for us, who can be against us?*

These words from the Old Testament book of Deuteronomy add a further dimension: "Let the beloved of the LORD rest secure in him, for he shields him all day long, and the one the LORD loves rests between his shoulders" (Deuteronomy 33:12). God literally invites us into His embrace, to rest our weary soul and body on His chest and experience "all Love can be" (theme song from the film, *A Beautiful Mind*). He invites us to do this after a long day of fighting *for* us. After defending and protecting us, He throws down His sword and shield, watches the enemy retreat in fear, wipes the sweat from His face, and beckons us to come near—to come near and understand that a fierce warrior can also possess love's tender touch.

What does it do to your heart to know that God has His eye on you like that? How does it change your perspective of Him to know that He does not send you into battle alone hoping that somehow you'll get through it? Does your heart skip a beat to realize that the Dread Warrior of Heaven will defend and protect you to this extent? How does it revolutionize your image of God to know that He will drop His sword and shield and allow you to feel His very heartbeat as you lay your head on His chest and rest between His shoulders?

When you peel back all the crusty layers of an impotent theology and years of empty religiosity, this is the kind of God that exists. This is the kind of God who, with His Son, Jesus, charged onto the bloody battlefield on our behalf. No, this was not pretty and it was not easy. In the midst of the horrors of a spiritual war, Jesus took a death blow, a terminal wound that sent the very earth into convulsions. Jesus did what He saw His Father doing down through the ages. And in the midst of it, He invites us into His embrace.

Recently I directed and participated in a spiritual retreat at The Jacob Institute. (Please refer to the end of this book for more information on The Jacob Institute.) As I walked the grounds of a local monastery on that cold and snowy day in February, I happened upon a sculptural rendition of the crucifixion that shocked me. It was the most striking portrayal of

Christ on the cross that I have ever witnessed. Most art forms that depict Christ's death leave Jesus looking rather, dare I say, wimpy. But this steel and metal interpretation communicated a much different Jesus—a brave and courageous Jesus with hands clutching the cross beams (palms in) with an arched back and chest protruding outward and upward. His face was pulled toward the heavens as He fought the good fight on my behalf. I could not take my eyes off Him for several minutes as tears streaked down my face. He is not only the God of all gods and the King of all kings, but He is also the Man of all men; the epitome of bravery and courage taking on the Enemy for me.

Somehow God is unfathomably drawn to my sharp and rough edges. He sees me and chooses to walk among the shards of glass to bind up my broken heart. My misty eyes become a window into my soul expressing naked vulnerability in the presence of my God who knows my dark side yet embraces me with unconditional intimacy. God promises His own in Jeremiah 24:7, "I will give them a heart to know me, that I am the LORD." God relentlessly pursues our hearts with this declaration: "I will give you a new heart and put a new spirit in you; I will remove your heart of stone and give you a heart of flesh" (Ezekiel 36:26). The apostle Paul echoes the same sentiments: "If anyone is in Christ, he is a new creation; the old is gone, the new has come! All this is from God who reconciled us to himself through Christ" (2 Corinthians 5:17-18).

A transformed heart is a heart that has been ravaged by the indescribable Divine Love. It is a heart that is able to declare that the old is gone and the new has arrived, that the False Self can be traded in for the True Self, that the skeletons in our closets can be buried for good. There is a reason the apostle John decided on the word "love" to identify God: "God is love. This is how God showed his love among us: He sent his one and only Son into the world that we might live through him. This is love: not that we loved God, but that he loved us and sent his Son as an atoning sacrifice for our sins" (1 John 4:8-10).

Love is not simply one of the many attributes of God. Love is the crucial cord that is woven through all His attributes. Love is the endearing quality that draws each of us to the heart of God. The apostle John was there at the foot of the cross. He watched the agony and anguish that sometimes accompanies love. He did not write the words in 1 John 4:8-10 as a result of research. He wrote them as a result of experience. In fact, John is described in the Scriptures as "the disciple whom Jesus loved." Does this mean Jesus didn't love the other disciples? No, because it's interesting to note that this description of John is found in the Gospel of... *John.* You guessed it, John described himself this way. It's not that John felt that he was the only disciple Jesus loved; the reality here is that John himself fully realized and felt that he was loved, and he was not afraid to declare that realization.

It's worth repeating: Love is not simply one of the many attributes of God; it is the crucial cord that weaves itself through all His attributes. Without love it is extremely difficult to be faithful. *Faithfulness without love is nothing more than obligation and duty.* Without love it is very hard to be just. The writer of Hebrews says that God disciplines those He loves. *Justice without love would result in cruel oppression.* Without love it is difficult to be all-powerful, because love is what motivated God to use His power to part the Red Sea and to send bread from heaven. Love is what motivated Jesus to heal the sick and miraculously feed hungry people. Love is what motivates Him now to walk with us through cancer, marital hardships, and painful memories. *Being all-powerful without love would result in tyranny.* Without love, God's holiness would seem uninviting. *Being holy without love would create an unfathomable distance in our relationship with Him.* Without love it is tough to be merciful, gracious, and compassionate because mercy, grace, and compassion naturally flow out of someone who is full of love. *Being merciful, gracious, and compassionate without love... well, doesn't even make sense.*

With that love comes fierce jealousy. "Do not worship any other god, for the LORD, whose name is Jealous, is a jealous God" (Exodus 34:14). His *name* is Jealous! Begin your next prayer with *that* name. God is ferociously jealous and furiously protective of us. This divine jealousy far exceeds the jealousy human beings exhibit. Do not confuse jealousy with envy. Envy involves wanting someone else's stuff. Jealousy, at its core, is relational. It's one of the important guards of any relationship. Jealousy is what enrages a man when he sees another man make advances toward his wife. Jealousy is what makes a wife ward off any flirtatious activity from another woman toward her husband. The main intention of jealousy is for it to burn so hot that it keeps other lovers, other gods, and other allurements from harming the relationship. Jealousy protects the core of the relationship and beats back anyone or anything that wishes to steal or harm the hearts of those in relation with each other. The reason we "burn with jealousy" when someone attempts to steal the heart of the one we love is because God's heart burns with jealousy; and we are created in His image. "Do not make for yourself an idol in the form of anything the LORD your God has forbidden. For the LORD your God is a *consuming fire*, a jealous God" (Deuteronomy 4:23-24, emphasis mine).

Think for a moment about what it would be like if jealousy were not a part of your closest, most intimate, relationships. You essentially would not care who or what came along to steal the heart, the time, and the affection of the one you love. And what if God were not jealous in His closest, most intimate relationships? He essentially would not care who or what came along to steal your heart, your time, and your affection. That type of god would be impotent to protect our very hearts from the deceitful allure of the Enemy.

What should be my response to such love? As a Christian, believe that you are truly accepted as one of God's own. Know that it's possible for you to be the recipient of unconditional love, even in your very unlovely condition. Enjoy the intimacy of a divine relationship. Contemplate that you are His beloved and the apple of His eye (Psalm 17:8). Know that as the other suitors are knocking on the door, He is jealously wooing you to His heart. This is the posture of the True Self. The True Self spends more time accepting God's love than living in the asinine excuses of why God shouldn't love you. The False Self lives in past blunders and hang-ups and refuses to come out from underneath their oppression. The False Self believes that the scars of the past serve as reasons why God cannot—should not—come close. In short, the True Self accepts love; the False Self refuses it.

The Scriptures give us insight into how men, women, boys, and girls can respond to the love of Christ. A love relationship with Jesus is as raw as a woman seeking Him out in a crowd just longing to touch a piece of His clothing. It's as adventurous as climbing a tree just to catch a glimpse of Him. It's as messy as crying your eyes out after you've betrayed Him. It's as fun as attending a wedding reception with never-ending new wine. It's as gut-wrenching as confessing adultery and murder. It's as practical as helping a fellow traveler get his donkey out of a ditch. It's as radical as pouring expensive perfume on His feet. It's as sensible as asking Him how to pray. It's as difficult as following Him wherever He goes. It's as uncomplicated as sitting at His feet and enjoying His company.

The disciple Philip requested that Jesus show him the Father, saying that would be enough. Jesus replied with a question: "Don't you know *me*, Philip, even after I have been among you for such a long time?" (John 14:9, emphasis mine). For approximately three years Philip had physically followed Jesus. He heard His words as demons were expunged from innocent people. He sought to understand as Jesus taught in parables. Philip saw with his own eyes miracles that ranged from creating wine without the lengthy fermentation process to healing a man from blindness with mud made from His own spittle. Yet Philip remained unaware, figuratively unconscious of the relationship Jesus was attempting to build with him and the truth He was trying to convey to him. The False Self is fine with spending time in spiritual activity, but steers clear of intimacy. We're alright being a part of the crowd that follows Jesus, but how do we respond when Jesus singles us out with a pointed question—*the single* question that reveals if we really know what's going on? I don't recall Philip saying much after that.

We often fail to step into what intimacy requires: openness, vulnerability, and a willingness to let God touch us in our deepest place. The False Self tends to say, "If Jesus could just show me," as if He were some magician that we are coaxing to reveal His secret. We would much rather practice what Doug Tell calls "folk religion." In his paper *Buddhism and Christianity: The Place Where the Two Faiths Meet*, he states, "Folk Christians might spend time reading the Bible, praying, fasting, or some other form of discipline, believing that God would be responsible to give some sort of blessing for the efforts he or she has made. They may go to church or give money, expecting God to respond by bringing some form of benefit, health or wealth into his or her life." He compares this to Folk Buddhism in which Buddhists basically do the same thing; they "manipulate the spirit world…in order to benefit his or her life," Tell says. Folk religion does not require anyone to give their heart away. Selfish manipulation and fear define the relational core of the False Self.

In contrast, David, the famous psalmist and Israel's most decorated warrior-king, is described as "a man after [God's] own heart" (1 Samuel 13:14). This life is not about manipulating God to secure a good life. It's about a heart connection with God. That's why David can ask with such great anticipation, "When can I go and meet with God?" (Psalm 42:2). His question drips with expectation and hope. His longing for God bubbles up from deep within his core because his heart has been captured by God's heart. David knew that an experience with God meant engagement at the heart level, a place where things are not easily explained, but incredibly profound.

9

The Voice of God

Finding God and our True Self involves pondering the utter mystique of the Scriptures. We must believe the unbelievable and allow the Voice of God to speak into our lives louder than any other voice. Frederick Buechner, in his book, *The Magnificent Defeat*, said this concerning the Bible: "If you really listen—and maybe you have to forget that it is the Bible being read and a minister who is reading it—there is no telling what you might hear."[1]

I have a vivid memory from my high school biology class. The sophomore year was the dissection year. Worms, large grasshoppers, frogs, and fetal pigs were pinned to large blocks of wax. Each team of dissectors was given the needed scalpels, tweezers, and scissors to begin the process of analyzing the innards of these little creatures. Some students were automatically given a hall pass in case they needed to make a run for the restroom. As I reflect back on that learning experience, I make this observation: When the animals were handed out, there were reactions and feelings of compassion, concern, and empathy for these dead things. When we saw the frog, we didn't just see a frog, we saw Kermit. When the pig was spread eagle in front of us, we didn't just see a pig, we remembered sweet little Wilbur from *Charlotte's Web*. But as the dissection continued our soft hearts became hardened. The compassion turned to callousness. With every cut the concern melted away, and by the end, we were throwing frog legs at each other. The worm, grasshopper, frog, and pig no longer looked like a worm, grasshopper, frog, and pig. They were basically piles of indistinguishable mutilated guts to which we had no emotional attachment. We clinically removed ourselves in order to perform the needed function. To have had too much empathy would have hindered the goal.

I have a fear that perhaps we have dissected the Scriptures, and consequently God, down to "ologies" and outlines that leave them and Him almost unrecognizable. Perhaps we have internalized our clinical distance when it comes to Scripture. We would rather dissect His Word than listen to His Voice. In an effort to find Him, we've lost Him. We tend to approach the Scriptures as a textbook, rather than God's autobiography. For years, to my shame, the Bible was no more exciting than standing in line to renew my driver's license. Doing *anything* with the Bible had become completely academic; it was fueled by duty instead of desire.

Just like we took the frog out of the pond and put it in the classroom, we've taken God out of the battlefield and put Him in the halls of academia. We've removed Him from the heavens and stuffed Him into our sermon outlines and between the covers of our books. We've taken Jesus from the dusty roads of Palestine where He made mud from his own spit to heal a blind man and attached words to him like *expiation* and *impeccability*. (It's as if a Greek dictionary isn't enough; now we need an English one.) Some of us who are Christ followers, have relegated Him to an hour on Saturday or Sunday. We've got Him where we want Him, and in the process of putting Him there, we have desensitized ourselves. The yearning for intimacy has melted away, while we throw doctrinal position papers at one another.

The Bible itself paints a much different picture, and to be honest, I'm not quite sure how we've missed it. Hebrews 4:12 is perhaps the most powerful description of the Word of God: "For the word of God is living and active. Sharper than any double-edged sword, it penetrates even to dividing soul and spirit, joints and marrow; it judges the thoughts and attitudes of the heart." According to Spiros Zodhiates, the word *living* in its original form means "to pass [on] one's life, from which is derived our word 'biography,' the narrative [or story] of how one spent his life."[2]

Let's unpack this concept of *living* a bit further. Genesis 2:7 says, "The LORD God formed man from the dust of the ground and *breathed into his nostrils the breath of life* and the man became a living being" (emphasis mine). Every human being alive today is breathing because of that initial burst of divine air that God breathed into Adam. John 20:22 says, "Jesus said, 'Peace be with you! As the Father has sent me, I am sending you.' And with that *he breathed on them* and said, 'Receive the Holy Spirit'" (emphasis mine). It's a bit odd to think about someone breathing on you. That's not something we go around doing to each other on a consistent basis. How did Jesus do it? Did He breathe on them like He was buffing His donkey's saddle or blowing out His birthday candles? I want you to think for a moment about the physical proximity in which you must be to another person for them to feel your breath. Close, very close indeed, intimately close! God breathed at the onset of human life. Jesus breathed on His closest followers, a most intimate way of bestowing His Spirit to them and communicating His peace and love for them.

Now listen closely to 2 Timothy 3:16: "All Scripture is *God-breathed*" (emphasis mine). The very lungs of God Himself cause the Scriptures to rise and fall, in and out, up and down. Scripture is God's way of getting close *to us* and revealing His heart. The same way He breathed life into Adam, He breathes life into us. As He got intimately close to His disciples and breathed on them, He wants to do the same with us. Are we close enough to feel His breath on our neck? In his preface to *The Pursuit of God*, A.W. Tozer said this:

> Sound Bible exposition is an imperative must in the Church of the Living God. Without it no church can be a New Testament church in any strict meaning of that term. But exposition may be carried on in such a way as to leave the hearers void of any true spiritual nourishment whatever. For it is not mere words that nourish the soul, but

God Himself, and unless the hearers find God in personal experience they are not the better for having heard the truth. The Bible is not an end in itself, but a means to bring men to an intimate and satisfying knowledge of God, that they may enter in Him, that they may delight in His Presence, may taste and know the inner sweetness of the very God Himself in the core and center of their hearts.[3]

Tozer wrote these words in the late 1940's on a train trip from Chicago to Texas. He was, perhaps, one crying in the wilderness, a man with enough courage to be the frontrunner in exposing a weakness in the modern approach to Christianity. It's what the post-modern Christian culture has been screaming for—an experiential knowing, a heart-transforming encounter with God.

The Word of God is not only living, it is sharper than any double-edged sword. It penetrates and divides not just joint and marrow, but soul and spirit. Remember the suggestion earlier that we've dissected the Scriptures and God down to something indistinguishable? In reality, it needs to be the other way around. God's Word is supposed to be dissecting us. It goes far beyond the physical, tangible world and pierces straight through to the intangible, spiritual realm. The *Word* (also used to describe Jesus in John 1) has a way of revealing and exposing my attitudes, my thoughts, my heart, my False Self, and my True Self. When I get close enough to feel His breath on me, there is a type of spiritual dissection that takes place that uncovers my deepest wounds, my greatest fears, my shameful thoughts, my inconsolable heartaches, my deplorable sins, my child-like faith, my appalling weaknesses, and every yearning of my soul.

Read carefully the following description of Jesus from Revelation 1:

I saw someone "like the son of man," dressed in a robe reaching down to his feet and with a golden sash around his chest. His head and hair were white like wool, as white as snow, and his eyes were like blazing fire. His feet were like bronze glowing in a furnace, and his voice was like the sound of rushing waters. In his right hand he held seven stars, *and out of his mouth came a sharp double-edged sword.* (Revelation 1:13-16, emphasis mine)

Here we see the riveting convergence that combines the person of Jesus and His mouth (words) with a sword. It's plain to see that when we read the Scriptures we are not simply opening a book, but we are engaging a Person.

Thomas C. Oden in *The Rebirth of Orthodoxy* stated, "The right reading of Scripture must be an act of obedience, praise, worship, and glory in the mystery of God revealed."[4] He continues, "Scripture must be allowed to speak for itself without our vested interests overbearing."[5] In other words, we need to keep our mouths shut and, for the moment, our commentaries closed. We need to keep our predisposed, biased, denominational views out of the equation and let God talk, let Him breath, let Him get close, let Him dissect us. When that happens, there's no telling what will take place to spiritually form our dingy, boring, apathetic, dutiful lives into lives really worth living, lives compelled by Christ's love.

M. Robert Mulholland, Jr. confesses something in his book *Shaped by the Word*: "I doubt if we ever really know completely and fully, in any sort of comprehensive way, exactly what God wants to do in our life at any given moment."[6] We *don't know* fully. This is why we lean in close and listen to Scripture as it unveils God's heart. We crave the Scripture because it reveals His intentions toward us, and somehow fills the void of unknowing just in time for another void to form, which keeps us on a continual search of a God who will never be fully known on this side of eternity.

Yet there seems to be a temptation toward the hyper-development of our analytical abilities at the expense of responding with the heart and spirit. Instead of craving the heart of God, I believe we've craved the intellectual process of trying to figure out what God has said in His Word. Obviously, we need our cognitive powers to process information, but a rational perspective alone toward the Scriptures neuters the unbelievable and mind-blowing facets represented in the Bible that can only be deciphered by and believed with the heart. If we are actually going to encounter God through the Scriptures, we must open ourselves at a deeper level to that possibility. The role of Scripture in Christian spirituality is to shape our hearts after God's own heart, thus enabling us to experience our True Self as we embody the Word. A failure to open up, to be touched at those deeper levels, to encounter, to engage, and to embody the Scripture is to remain firmly rooted in our False Self.

One of the key components to this mystery of embodying the Scripture and consequently living from our True Self is found in this question: *What might it look like if we really took seriously the gospel that we have discovered and experienced in and through the Scriptures?* This is a question that was asked routinely by one of my graduate level professors, and it's a haunting question for several reasons. First, it jerks us out of our spiritual daydreams, our apathetic routines, our undisturbed lives, our polite existences, and asks, "So, how serious are you about what you have encountered?"

Secondly, this question allows the Scripture to beg entrance into our lives and not simply be words on a page, a plaque on the wall, or cards in a memory packet.

Thirdly, I believe this question inquires into how serious we are about God in general. Since God and His Word are so intricately tied together, we cannot accept one and reject the other. To the Jews who persecuted Him in John 5, Jesus said, "You diligently study the Scriptures because you think that by them you possess eternal life. These are the Scriptures that testify about me, yet you refuse to come to me to have life" (John 5:39-40). The travesty is to study the Scriptures and remain distant from the Triune God. We play charades by creating a lot of movement, yet accomplishing little in regards to the Kingdom of God. The answer to this question determines the height, breadth, and depth of our journey as a disciple of Jesus. How far will we go? What dangers are we willing to encounter? What are we willing to leave? Who are we willing to leave? Who are we willing to call our family? What boat are we willing to step out of? Are we willing to have our identity affirmed, tested, and developed? Can we step outside our kingdom to live whole-heartedly in the Kingdom of God?

The haunting weightiness continues with Mulholland's description of what it means to be "uncovered and laid bare" in God's sight from Hebrews 4. It is to be "naked...laid back...exposed...across the knee of the victor with throat exposed"[7] as in the case of a surrendered gladiator or sacrificial lamb. This is complete vulnerability. The role of Scripture in personal spiritual formation is to lovingly bend each of us into this position. We naturally tend to place ourselves defensively against God in blatant and subtle ways. To imagine this "cut throat" posture across the altar of sacrifice or the knee of God is indeed frightening, yet it's exactly what we want. The intense pain of vulnerability toward God is not half as painful as a life lived with a stiff neck and arms folded firmly across the chest—the posture of the False Self.

Are you willing to let God touch you at your deepest level? Am I? I have seen far too much of the opposite: people who live a life in which Scripture glances off their external façade. We read words like "Do not store up for yourselves treasures on the earth," then down our last sip of coffee before heading to work for 60-70 hours a week so we can pursue the American Dream. How can we be so woefully unaware that we have deep places within us that God wants to penetrate with His Word? Jesus said, "Everyone who hears these words of mine and does not put them into practice is like a foolish man who built his house on sand. The rain came down, the streams rose, and the winds blew and beat against that house, and it fell with a great crash" (Matthew 7:26-27). I am painfully ignorant that Scripture is meant to be taken seriously. I am so busy building my little house on the sand that the thought of a "cut-throat" posture seems a bit overdone and melodramatic.

It is not what we *do* with Scripture that spiritually forms us. It is what God, through Scripture, does to us as we listen to and heed the Voice of God with a sincere and vulnerable heart.

[1] Frederick Buechner, *The Magnificent Defeat* (New York: HarperCollins, 1985), p. 10.

[2] Spiros Zodhiates, editor, *The Complete Word Study Dictionary: New Testament* (Iowa Falls, IA: World Bible Publishers, 1992), p. 697.

[3] Aiden Wilson Tozer, The Pursuit of God (1948. Reprint. Camp Hill: Wing Spread Publishers, 1982, 1993), p. 9.

[4] Thomas C. Oden, *The Rebirth of Orthodoxy* (New York: HarperCollins, 2003), p. 102.

[5] Ibid, p. 104.

[6] M. Robert Mulholland, Jr., *Shaped by the Word* (Nashville: Upper Room Books, 2000), p. 15

[7] Ibid, p. 40.

10

The Intimacy of Prayer

In *Mere Christianity* C. S. Lewis said that "the moment you wake up each morning, all your wishes and hopes for the day rush at you like wild animals. And the first job each morning consists in shoving it all back; in listening to that other voice, taking that other point of view, letting that other, larger, stronger, quieter life come flowing in."[1] Yes, the quieter life. A life of solitude that engages in a conversation that reinforces "that other point of view." Prayer is, as one unknown author put it, "the unembarrassed interchange of thoughts, love, ideas, and desire." It is, in one simple word, a conversation. It's a give and take, throwing the ball back and forth, talking, listening, sharing, laughing, crying, and communicating. Prayer itself is an intimate act, yet many of us are not willing to be that intimate because *intimacy requires something of us*. When we're willing to give ourselves over to the relationship, prayer then reaches the depths of intimacy.

Prayer is sometimes called a spiritual discipline, only because we are not always up to what it takes to make a relationship work. Communication is innate, intrinsic, inborn, and a part of the very fiber of any relationship. You don't *have* a relationship if there is no communication. Look around. Marriage relationships fall apart and die for lack of communication. The relationships between parents and their teenagers take a sabbatical for years at a time because no one talks. Employers and employees live in tension-filled silence because no one wants to speak up. No one in these aforementioned relationships wants to make a significant deposit into the relationship through an unembarrassed interchange of thoughts, love, ideas, and desire.

John Eldredge said, "Relationship requires things of me that are harder than a life of comfortable distance."[2] This is why the Story took a fatal turn not far into the written account. Genesis 3 tells us that God was taking his usual stroll in the garden in the cool of the day, probably wanting to spend some time with Adam and Eve and engage in conversation. He was looking for them and asked, "Where are you?" It was not an angry voice, but the voice of a concerned parent who could not find the child He loved so dearly.

> Then the man and his wife heard the sound of the LORD God as he was walking in the garden in the cool of the day, and they hid from the LORD God among the trees of the garden. But the LORD God called to the man, "Where are you?" (Genesis 3:8-9)

Where were they? They were at a comfortable distance. They were hiding. They were embarrassed, and rightly so, for they had just defied the one boundary God gave them. They sewed fig leaves together to cover their naked bodies and hid among the trees. This was the first form of camouflage, and we proudly wear our fig leaves today that hide us and keep us at a comfortable distance. Our jobs, our hobbies, our hang-ups, our addictions, and our personalities act as fig leaves that create and solidify the False Self. These fig leaves keep us from engaging in an honest conversation that truly reveals what is really beneath our surface. You see, we want the relationship; we just don't want the work it takes to have one.

God wants us to talk (as well as listen). He wants us to be that annoying little kid that just won't shut up. Jesus said that "unless you change and become like little children, you will never enter the kingdom of heaven" (Matthew 18:3). Our humility, our openness, our transparency, our emotion, our simple faith, our lack of fear, and our talkativeness—God wants it all.

"Call to me and I will answer you," says the LORD, "and tell you great and unsearchable things you do not know" (Jeremiah 33:3). *Really? Is this your experience with God?* Every time you dial, He picks up and has this boatload of wonderful and glorious things to talk to you about? I'm going to go out on a limb and say that this is rare, but not because God isn't holding up His end of the deal. It's because we don't expect or want that kind of intimacy, that kind of a conversation. As they say, it's all in the approach, and more often than not, we approach God through prayer much like handing Him our weekly grocery list. *Here's what I need, God. See what You can do about it.*

If prayer is an "unembarrassed interchange of thoughts, love, ideas, and desire," what does it look like? Psalm 139 is an "unembarrassed interchange" with God.

> O LORD, you have searched me and you know me. You know when I sit and when I rise; you perceive my thoughts from afar. You discern my going out and my lying down; you are familiar with all my ways. (Psalm 139:1-3)

Prayer reaches the depths of intimacy when you have *nothing to hide.* Is it possible to approach God as the old hymn writer suggested: naked, helpless, and empty-handed? *Search me, know me, track me down, Lord. Ask where I've been, God. You know anyway. You know the rhythms of my day. Come looking for me even when I'm hiding.* The True Self is not afraid to be found. The False Self, however, takes offense at Divine intrusion. Do you welcome God's omniscience and omnipresence, or does it unnerve you?

> Before a word is on my tongue, you know it completely. (Psalm 139:4)

Do you know couples who have been together for so long that they finish one another's sentences? The ultimate indication that intimacy is taking place is when the Lord finishes my sentences for me. He knows the rhythm of my prayers and the manner in which I pour out my heart. Prayer becomes intimate when my words and the sound of my voice become so familiar to Him *that He knows what I'm going to say.*

> You hem me in—behind and before; you have laid your hand upon me. Such knowledge is too wonderful for me, too lofty for me to attain. Where can I go from your Spirit? Where can I flee from your presence? If I go up to the heavens, you are there; if I make my bed in the depths, you are there. If I rise on the wings of the dawn, if I settle on the far side of the sea, even there your hand will guide me, your right hand will hold me fast. (Psalm 139:5-10)

Prayer becomes an intimate conversation when you have *nowhere else to go.* God is everywhere you turn. When He is in the midst of your depression, your anger, your frustration, your joy, your happiness, your contentment, your discontentment, your anxiety, and your fear, then you have reached a deeper level of intimacy. When you realize God is everywhere you turn and that you cannot hide in the trees of your personality or your past, you are intimately communing with the One whose right hand is always touching you. The True Self invites this type of invasion into its personal space. The False Self interprets this kind of closeness much like a prisoner interacts with the warden.

> For you created my inmost being; you knit me together in my mother's womb. I praise you because I am fearfully and wonderfully made; your works are wonderful, I know that full well. My frame was not hidden from you when I was made in the secret place. When I was woven together in the depths of the earth, your eyes saw my unformed body.

All the days ordained for me were written in your book before one of them came to be. (Psalm 139:13-16)

Prayer becomes an intimate conversation when you *accept yourself as God sees you.* Instead of the False Self asking, "Why, Lord?" the True Self says, "Thanks, Lord." Instead of bemoaning the day you were born or wishing for death, you realize the sovereign control God has over your life. Intimacy requires acceptance and trust of the One who loves us, and if we don't see ourselves the way God sees us, we will forever hold Him at arms' length.

How precious to me are your thoughts, O God! How vast is the sum of them! Were I to count them, they would outnumber the grains of sand. When I awake, I am still with you. (Psalm 139:17-18)

Prayer becomes an intimate conversation when you *actually care what God thinks.* This is when you ask Him questions without already knowing what you want Him to say. It's asking for discernment or wisdom in a decision without any biases of your own. It's treasuring the thoughts and mind of God so much that the questions we ask Him *require us to listen.* We often rattle off a one-sided speech to God and then fail to "be still" and know that He *is* God. We fail to turn our head and listen for that still small voice, that gentle whisper. We fail to quiet ourselves in solitude, away from the noise of the world so we can sense the movement of the Holy Spirit in us.

I've gotten into a habit when I meet with someone over lunch or breakfast for a conversation. On my way to the appointment I simply ask, "God, what do You want me to say to so-and-so today? What do they need to hear?" You see, that requires me to listen. If I were to piously pray, "Gaaaawd, guide this conversation by Your grace and mercy," well, that kind of prayer does not require me to listen. Get into the habit of asking God questions that require you to listen for an answer. *God, do You want us to buy this car?* Not, *God, stop us if You don't want us to buy this car.* Do you see the difference?

Lest you think I have a special direct line to God that you don't have, let me say this: when I listen for God, I have never heard an audible voice. Some people say they have and I will not argue with them. God is capable of doing anything He wants. I do, however, hear Him through His written Word. I hear Him through certain senses and inklings I have as I try to keep in step with the Spirit. (Please note that if you are intentionally, or even ignorantly, not walking in the Spirit, the senses and inklings in your soul may not be a good standard by which to live.) I hear Him through my spiritual friends. I hear Him through sacred literature. I hear and see Him in nature. I especially sense His presence and quiet whisper in silence and solitude. However, listening to and hearing God takes discernment. Discernment is the ability to recognize the difference between the Voice and patterns of God, the voice and patterns of the Enemy, and our own voice and natural tendencies. Discernment only comes when we are teachable and willing to hear whatever God might say without our personal biases creating spiritual static. At this point I need to be very clear about this extremely delicate issue of hearing God. When friends say that "God told them" something, ninety-nine percent of the time it tracks with Scripture. *God told me to call a friend and encourage her. God prompted me to pray for so-and-so. God told me that He loved me. I think God wants us to go to Colorado on vacation. God spoke to me and said that He was grieved by my anger and bitterness.* All of these statements coincide with God's written Word. Not one of them goes against the Scriptural grain. I get nervous when cults are formed after "hearing" from God. I'm uneasy when heresy blossoms and is linked to someone "hearing" from God. I'm unsettled when someone uses God's words as an excuse to live their own agenda. After David compliments God on how wonderful His thoughts are, he continues with this:

If only you would slay the wicked, O God! Away from me, you bloodthirsty men! They speak of you with evil intent; your adversaries misuse your name. Do I not hate those who hate you, O LORD, and abhor those who rise up against you? I have nothing but hatred for them; I count them my enemies. (Psalm 139:19-22)

Prayer becomes an intimate conversation when *you can talk to God like that!* Prayer is not always polite, not always pretty, not always poetic or romantic. Sometimes it's raw and edgy and uncomfortably honest. An intimate conversation with God runs the gamut of emotions and brings our truest feelings and our True Self to the surface. It makes absolutely no sense to wear a mask while praying because God can see through it anyway.

Thomas à Kempis, the late medieval monk who wrote *The Imitation of Christ* went through a particularly dark time in his life and was convinced that God was not present with him. At one point there was a showdown and Thomas cried out to God in the darkness, "If you absent yourself one more time, I'll break every commandment in the book!"[3] No mask there. Our raw feelings need God's intimate touch.

Search me, O God, and know my heart; test me and know my anxious thoughts. See if there is any offensive way in me, and lead me in the way everlasting. (Psalm 139:23-24)

Prayer breeds intimacy when you *can honestly acknowledge your shadow side and follow God's lead.* At the beginning of this psalm, David *acknowledged* that God searches him. Now David gives God *permission.* God doesn't *need* our permission, but there is something that happens inside our inner being when we give Him permission to roam the corridors of our heart to cleanse those offensive ways in us. And how do we respond to this inner cleansing, this Divine Intrusion? We ask Him to lead the way and, in turn, we follow.

The False Self is more comfortable following at a distance. There are certain things required in this Divine relationship that he or she will not venture into. Intimacy feels like an infringement instead of a connection. Prayer feels more like a chore than the intimate bond it is meant to be.

The True Self comes close and slowly unveils. In all the nervousness and modesty of a virgin bride on her honeymoon night, the True Self gives herself (or himself) over fully to the Bridegroom. The touch is tender. The conversation is intimate and reassuring. The uneasiness subsides as God assures us that, even with all our flaws and insecurities, He loves and accepts us beyond our ability to comprehend.

---

[1] C.S. Lewis, *The Complete C.S. Lewis Signature Classics* (New York: Harper-Collins, 2002), p. 167.

[2] John Eldredge, *Developing a Conversational Intimacy with God,* compact disc (Colorado Springs: Ransomed Heart).

[3] William Griffin, "Figures in the Fog: Thomas a Kempis on Discernment," Conversations Volume 6:2 (2008): p 77.

11

Often I feel as though I'm viewing the world as an outsider looking in, wondering if there really could be something to this whole *Matrix* concept. The sacred writings say that "the whole world is under the control of the evil one," (1 John 5:19) but the average Christian lives as if this is just a good Hollywood storyline rather than a biblical statement of reality. The 2010 film *Inception* dared to tackle this topic regarding the inability to live in reality. If I were to sum up the secondary plot (or perhaps the spiritual plot) of the main character in the story it would be this: It reveals the struggle to live in reality, the laborious effort to find and remain in what is real instead of getting tangled in layer upon layer of what is not real. When we consistently live in layer upon layer of what is not real, we become increasingly disoriented toward what is real. And that, my friend, is a very dangerous place. For those of you who saw the film, at the end we were left wondering if Dom's totem stopped spinning. We were left to wonder if he was in his own reality. I have the same wonderment for most of us who travail on this earth. Are we living in accordance with reality, or are we fooling ourselves by creating an alternate state of being—a dream world, if you will—where we continue to carry out the plot of the False Self?

"Man is a mere phantom as he goes to and fro; he bustles about, but only in vain" (Psalm 39:6). Humankind has always possessed the talent of hustling and bustling about in futility. Just go to a shopping mall at Christmas and you'll see what I mean. The Teacher from Ecclesiastes observes from the empirical evidence that "everything is meaningless" (Ecclesiastes 1:2). He experimented with everything under the sun (legitimate pleasure, hard work, women, riches, folly) and concluded that the most important facet in life is to "fear God and keep his commandments, for this is the whole duty of man" (Ecclesiastes 12:13). Of course, "there is a time for everything" (Ecclesiastes 3:1) in a person's life. Life is not void of things to do, people to see, and places to go. However, if we are not careful, the reality of life can slip ever so subtly into a state of perpetual "me." And when life becomes all about little ol' me, everything begins to feel meaningless. We were made for more, so much more, than simply fulfilling our own myopic desires.

The fear of Isaac

Jacob was not only the perpetrator when it came to the manipulation of others for his own benefit, he was also a victim. His father-in-law, Laban (who was also his uncle!), played with him like a cat plays with a wounded mouse. Laban always seemed to have the upper hand over Jacob because Laban knew what Jacob wanted—one of his daughters. Therefore, Laban batted Jacob back and forth at will. He eked 20 years of hard labor out of Jacob simply because he could. Laban's power and control were rooted in Jacob's longing for Rachel. I have got to hand it to Jacob; what a man won't do for love! He first endured a back-handed comment from his future father-in-law that would have made any respectable man cock his head. After Jacob made known his desire to wed Rachel, the younger of Laban's daughters, Laban replied, "It's better that I give her to you than some other man" (Genesis 29:19). In other words, *Eh, I guess you are no more of a jerk than all those other guys. I guess I'll give her to you.* But this was just the beginning.

Jacob honorably worked hard for Laban for seven years in order to receive Rachel as his wife. At the end of this agreed period of time, Jacob requested his payment. Laban threw a huge party and proceeded to play off Jacob's ignorance of family and societal customs. Unknown to Jacob, underneath all the wedding veils was Leah, the older daughter with "weak eyes." (The custom was to marry off the oldest daughter first.) This is still somewhat unfathomable to me, but the story reveals that Jacob made love to Leah that first night without realizing it *was* Leah. Maybe he had weak eyes, too! The next morning Jacob realized with whom he had slept and proceeded, with good reason, to blow a gasket and question why Laban had done such a thing. I wonder if at any point Jacob was haunted by flashbacks of his own deception with his father Isaac.

Laban calmed down the boy by assuring him that if he finished out the bridal week with Leah that he would immediately give him Rachel as his second wife in return for another seven years of labor. And so it happened. Within the course of a week, Jacob ended up with two wives, but remained in the services of Laban for another seven years.

But Jacob had at least one trick left up his sleeve. When he requested that Laban release him from his fulfilled 14-year obligation, Laban became a bit concerned that the blessing that Jacob had brought to his household and flocks would leave with him. You see, Jacob had turned out to be a kind of lucky rabbit's foot to Laban. Jacob agreed to continue to shepherd Laban's flocks, but requested payment in the form of every spotted and speckled sheep, every dark-colored lamb, and every spotted and speckled goat. Laban would keep the non-spotted and non-speckled ones. Jacob then proceeded with one of the most elaborate and contrived farming scandals in agricultural history. I still don't completely understand the gimmickry described in Genesis 30:37-43, but Jacob, over the course of six years, ended up producing quite a herd of strong spotted and speckled goats for himself! "So the weak animals went to Laban and the strong ones to Jacob" (Genesis 30:42). Call it Goat-Gate, I guess. Later, in chapter 31, Jacob even gives God credit for all this, claiming that the Lord had revealed this mating procedure in a dream. Honestly, I wish I had more of the story to go on here. I want to believe him, but I'm having a little difficulty buying everything Jacob is selling.

Nonetheless, Jacob got the cue from God to head home, but he failed to inform Laban of his intentions. Laban pursued Jacob, caught up with him, and asked why he skipped town so quickly. To be honest, I can see why Jacob wanted to get out from under Laban's thumb. Even as Laban gazed at everything Jacob had—his wives, his children, and his spotted and speckled goats—he claimed, "All you see is mine" (Genesis 31:43). I realize Jacob had manipulated the whole goat herd to his advantage, but Laban was still a bit deluded in his assessment that everything was his! After a heated conversation, both Jacob and Laban made a truce—you won't hurt me anymore and I won't hurt you anymore. "So Jacob took an oath in the name of *the Fear* of his father Isaac" (Genesis 31:53 – emphasis mine).

The Fear. In my imagination I see Jacob beginning to come to grips with the weight of his life. His False Self just got spooked, and he invoked a little-used name for God—"the Fear of Isaac" (Genesis 31:42). Two times in the course of this confrontation with Laban, Jacob revealed an intimate family name for Yahweh—the Fear. He spoke a name that made known what was at the core of his father Isaac, and what may just have been forming inside his own heart even then. Isaac had good reason to perceive God a bit differently than everyone else. As a boy he endured the frightful experience of almost being offered as a child sacrifice by his father Abraham. Abraham was being tested by God in order to find out if he truly loved and feared Yahweh above all else, even his own son. You see, child sacrifice was not uncommon in this ancient culture. But Yahweh proved Himself completely different, completely set apart, completely Other than all the other gods to whom parents would offer their children in death. While other gods, such as Molech, would consume children through fire every time, the God of Abraham stopped the execution as a way of saying two very important things: "Now I know that you *fear* God, because you have not withheld from me your son, your only son" (Genesis 22:12, emphasis mine), and *I'm not like all those other gods.*

Isaac was indelibly marked by the mercy of God. I imagine there was not a day after during which he did not think about that profound God-encounter. So great was the impact, that he and God shared between them a special name—the Fear. In some way Isaac passed down not only the name, but the concept of "the Fear" to Jacob. And so from the recesses of Jacob's True Self, he was considering if he should, as his father did, view God in the same way.

The Fear describes a God who can demand everything, take you to the brink, and come through like no one else can. The Fear speaks of a reverential awe so profound that it serves as a weighty wake-up call to our slumbering conscience. The Fear describes a Deity that is totally Other, supremely Holy, and unquestionably Worthy. The Fear speaks of a daily personal awareness of God that goes light years beyond what we may have learned in a theology class. The Fear creates a contemplative dimension to the human soul that makes life an honor to live, not a right. The Fear changes our narrow-minded perception about life as we know it and starts to form within us a spiritual sense that there is more going on than what our feeble minds can fathom. The Fear sends us to our knees in worship and flattens us prostrate before His Presence. And the Fear picks us up off the altar with a renewed and intense experiential knowledge of the personification of Mercy and Grace. You see, Isaac did not leave Mount Moriah that day simply fearing God; he left *knowing the Fear.* He descended that mountain with a new stream running deep in his soul.

We have lost that. I have lost that. During life's hustle and bustle we have failed to be still long enough to realize just how out of touch we are with a God called the Fear. We play our church games and our Facebook games and our video games to the near total neglect of what it means to submit ourselves to the Fear; to lie there on the altar without a fight and trust that what is happening comes from a God who can do no wrong. Our vain, meaningless, and egocentric life is the new normal. We expect nothing more. Our closest interaction with God may be a few hurried moments flipping through a devotional book or attending a church service where God is presented more as the Fun than the Fear. To approach God as the Fear, to live in the presence of God as the Fear, is to question every thought we think, every action we follow through with, every motive that every action is born out of, and every word we utter. It would mean that we bring our entire life under the knee-buckling and awesome gaze of the Fear. It would mean losing my life in order to find it, just like Isaac. It would mean sacrificing our False Selves and all the accompanying comforters, so that "we too may live a new life" (Romans 6:4). The Fear's gaze is piercing, but life-giving; terrifying, but merciful; bone-crushing, but tender. Under the gaze of the Fear the False Self crumbles and our True Self is raised.

I truly wish you could sense the deep angst in my heart and hear the inflection of these words as if I were speaking them. My heart is heavy that we have somehow skirted many opportunities to not only find, but once we have found, to actually engage this God that we "so blithely invoke"[1] (in the words of Annie Dillard). What would our churches do if the Fear showed up on Sunday morning? I dare say we are absolutely unprepared to deal with the majesty and mystery of the Fear if He were to grace us with His Presence. "Tremble, O earth, at the presence of the Lord, at the presence of the God of Jacob" (Psalm 114:7). "Serve the LORD with fear and rejoice with trembling" (Psalm 2:11). "Worship the LORD in the splendor of his holiness. Tremble before him, all the earth!" (1 Chronicles 16: 29-30). When was the last time I *trembled* before God? Regrettably, I have no idea.

A crossroads

"This what the LORD says: 'Stand at the crossroads and look; ask for the ancient paths, ask where the good way is, and walk in it, and you will find rest for your souls'" (Jeremiah 6:16). We would rather barrel through the crossroads at high speed looking for the next bigger and better thing to satiate the False Self. We would rather go on an all-out search for that golden ticket that will miraculously bring sense to our lives. Some of us would rather pull off onto the shoulder and sit with the engine idling, gripped by fear by what we might hear God say if we were to stop at the intersection and ask about the good way and ancient path. Who wants to "inch forward on filaments of hope"? Who wants to stand at the crossroads to ponder, look, contemplate, and *ask* which way is the right way? That just seems old-school.

As a means of parenthesis, let me take this one paragraph to say that we must not completely sub-contract out our spiritual formation to our church's or denomination's ministry strategy. (I say this not only as an author, but also as a pastor who has strategized much about ministry whether I wanted to or not.) Call it what you may—liturgy, ministry strategy, discipleship program, confirmation classes, Christian education, mission, vision—these all have their place in the unique environment of your church, but we must not blindly hand over our heart and spiritual formation to anyone but Jesus. Each of us, individually, must stand at the crossroads and take personal responsibility for how we are caring for, feeding, and guarding this treasure we call the heart. The driven nature of our current early-21st-century American culture has assaulted each of us. The arteries of our hearts are clogged with busyness, noise, compulsiveness, debt, depression, and yes, even inadequate religious systems that sometimes, albeit unintentionally, blur the Gospel and misdirect the sheep.

God has orchestrated many crossroads in my life. I'm sure He has in yours, too. Have I recognized them all as spiritual rest stops at which I should slow down and ponder anew what the ancient, good way is? No, not every time. Do you see the absolute beauty in God providing crossroads for us? They are planned times of rest, re-evaluation, and a fresh navigation of the mysterious territory of the heart. What may seem a nuisance just may be a critical juncture in your desperate journey of finding God and your True Self. It doesn't mean you *have* to turn right or left. It simply means that you fear, respect, and love God enough to slow down, stop, and ask. Sometimes these crossroads will come sooner than you think they should. You may be fine with cruising along as normal, but God wants you to slow down, stand, look, and ask about the good and ancient way.

Which path encourages you to crucify your False Self and allows your True Self to be raised to life? Which way allows your heart to come alive and for you to fall deeper in love with Jesus? Which way makes you look most like an authentic fumbling, bumbling apprentice of Jesus? Which way allows Christ to be conceived and formed in you? If God says to proceed straight, then proceed straight. If He says the good and ancient way is now to the left, then turn left. Ask Him now: *Lord, what is the good and ancient way?*

I can tell you now that this is not easy. If fact, I omitted the last part of Jeremiah 6:16 till now: "But you said, 'We will not walk in it.'" There seems to be a human stubbornness that sometimes trumps the clear Voice of God. Yet the gift of personal choice is one of God's most precious gifts to us, and He will not take that from us.

True reality is when we listen to the Voice of God and then proceed accordingly. It matters not if the road is smooth or rough. It matters not if the weather is sunny or stormy. It matters only that God is with us and for us. And since He *is* for us, who can stand against us?

---

[1] http://www.inwardoutward.org/author/annie-dillard

The Grand Crescendo

Out of sheer gratitude for never leaving me to face my perils alone, I have composed this contemporary psalm as a sacrifice of praise.

Mighty God,
Your fame is unmatched
Your sheer and utter holiness brings me to my knees
Overwhelm me with Your renown
Engulf me with Your marvels
Surround me with Your presence
Enfold me with Your peace
Capture me with Your beauty

Your transcendence radiates from all creation
Your distinction sets You apart as knowable, yet unknowable
Saturate the dry places of my heart
Peel away my hard encrusted external facade
Gently seep into the inner places of my soul
Tenderly draw me to Your heart
Heal me in the deepest, remotest corners of my being

Your Son's blood proves You will go to great lengths to win me back
Your holiness sets the boundaries of my freedom
Drench me with Your intense love
Purify me with Your grace, mercy, and forgiveness
Gently lift me when I stumble

Bury my sinful atrocities in the depths
Enthusiastically throw a party upon my return

Your power knows no limit
Your Spirit knows no boundary
Guide me on intimate walks and breath-taking adventures
Softly hold me to Your chest so that I may hear Your heart
Courageously roam the corridors of my heart and mind
Shake up the complacent tendencies of my False Self
Constantly assure me that my heart is new

Your ancient and good ways bring my True Self to life
Your utter acceptance of me based on profound love and simple faith is simply
unbelievable
Clear up my distorted and warped image of You
Forgive me for my stubbornness and stiff neck
Settle my soul as I attempt to know the Fear
Dance with me when I catch glimpses of who You truly are
And please, please, even so, come quickly, Lord Jesus

About The Jacob Institute

Do you want to continue this journey of finding God and your True Self? The Jacob Institute partners with you in your spiritual formation by offering spiritual resources and opportunities in the forms of spiritual retreats, spiritual direction, small groups, and a non-accredited Certificate of Spiritual Formation Program through The Spiritual Formation Academy.

Jamie Overholser is the founder and director of The Jacob Institute.

For more information please go to our website at
www.thejacobinstitutecsf.org or write us at

The Jacob Institute of Christian Spiritual Formation
PO Box 523
Clarks Summit, PA 18411

About the Author

Jamie Overholser is a fumbling, bumbling apprentice of Jesus whose passion is to see Christ formed in others. He received his M.A. in Spiritual Formation and Leadership from Spring Arbor University (Spring Arbor, MI). He is the founder and director of **The Jacob Institute of Christian Spiritual Formation** which focuses on *Finding God and your True Self* through spiritual retreat. Jamie is married to his beautiful wife Julie and has 4 amazing children. He loves the beach and enjoys riding his Honda Rebel.

Author photograph by Shades of Gray Photography (www.shadesofgraypa.com)